Contents

Introduction

Citizenship is set to play an increasingly important part in the curriculum, across all key stages. As authors of this book we feel it is vital that citizenship is taught in both discreet and discrete ways from as early a stage as possible in schools. This book develops many of the approaches we used in *Ideas for Citizenship: Key Stage 1*, as well as tackling a number of areas which may be better suited to older children. At Key Stage 2, many challenging notions can be introduced and explored, before they are considered in more depth and breadth in subsequent key stages.

The National Curriculum handbook for teachers ('Curriculum 2000') talks of helping to 'give pupils the knowledge, skills and understanding they need to… become informed, active, responsible citizens.' In writing this book, and whilst addressing this statement, we aim also to help teachers enable children to become questioning and thinking citizens. We hope that both teachers and children become more reflective learners as they study citizenship.

About this book

The activities in this book can help all teachers deliver both what is appropriate for their particular circumstances and what the government advises. Obviously not all schools are the same, and there will be many different approaches to the teaching of citizenship. This book, however, endorses its teaching in ways which help the whole school community embrace the ideas inherent in the subject area, and promotes the subject as a way of thinking, rather than simply a collection of teachable facts.

Many of the activities in these pages have clear, identifiable outcomes. Others are a starting point for ongoing discussion within the classroom, and the wider school community, about what it means to be a citizen in the twenty-first century.

The activity learning objectives adhere closely to the citizenship non-statutory guidelines of the National Curriculum. The section headings in this book, however, are our own and reflect what we believe are the most significant areas within the subject. Teaching citizenship often involves having to tackle difficult issues and the hope is that in all the sections teachers will find new, stimulating ideas to equip them to be able to deal with such issues with sensitivity and confidence. The activities can be developed and the teacher's own slant added to them over time.

Each activity follows the same format. There are learning objectives and cross-curricular links (and the thinking teacher will surely find more), a list of the resources needed to teach the activity and how best to organise the classroom, where appropriate. There then follows a short introduction for the teacher's benefit, and a detailed explanation of how to conduct the activity. The conclusion offers prompts to stimulate the children in reflecting on the learning. The 'Now or later' section is very important, offering suggestions for follow-up work in the classroom, the wider school community and sometimes as possible homework activities.

Ideas for citizenship Key Stage 1

The activities in *Ideas for Citizenship: Key Stage 1* are arranged under similar section headings as those in this book. The progression between the two books is obvious and natural. It may be that some activities in this book are easily adapted for the younger age group, and similarly some of the Key Stage 1 activities may be suitable for certain children in Years 3 and 4.

Ready to go!

IDEAS FOR CITIZENSHIP

KS2

P4 to 7

AUTHORS
Emily Feldberg and Rob Walton

EDITOR
Dulcie Booth

ASSISTANT EDITOR
Christine Harvey

SERIES DESIGNER
Anna Oliwa

DESIGNER
Erik Ivens

ILLUSTRATIONS
Bill Houston

COVER ARTWORK
Andy Parker

Designed using Adobe Pagemaker
Published by Scholastic Ltd, Villiers House, Clarendon Avenue, Leamington Spa, Warwickshire CV32 5PR
Printed by Bell & Bain Ltd, Glasgow

1234567890 2345678901

British Library Cataloguing-in-Publication Data
A catalogue record for this book is available from the British Library.

ISBN 0-590-53473-4

EMILY'S DEDICATION
For the trainee teacher students of Sunderland drama specialism class 2000 who wanted resources. Hope this helps! Now you can change the world...

ROB'S DEDICATION
To Mum and Dad, with love and thanks.

ACKNOWLEDGEMENTS
The Health Development Agency for information based on the leaflets 'Think about Drink' and 'Drugs – the facts'.

Save The Children Fund UK for text based on the UN Convention on the Rights of the Child, 1989.

The Controller of HMSO and the Queen's Printer for Scotland for material quoted from The National Curriculum © Crown copyright material.

Every effort has been made to trace copyright holders and the publishers apologise for any inadvertent omissions.

Section 1

Research, discuss and debate

The ability to question and evaluate information is vital if children are to become active, thinking citizens. The activities in this section aim to equip children with the skills of assessing, questioning and using information in debate and discussion. This section also addresses those citizenship guidelines that state that children should be able to share their opinions and explain their views. Alongside these skills the children should develop an awareness that people hold different opinions and that it is important to respect these differences.

Shades of opinion

Resources and classroom organisation

You will need: the phrases *I agree* _________ *because...* and *but I don't agree* _________ *because...* written on two large prompt cards; flip chart or board; writing materials.

At some point you will need to set up a class discussion circle with chairs.

Introduction

One of the most important areas of citizenship is being able to discuss and exchange views with other people. Talk frames help children to discuss issues in any subject areas and once practised and mastered will develop their skills in discussion, debate, and justifying and explaining their views.

What to do

Explain to the children that when we discuss something it is important to realise that sometimes we may disagree with some parts of another person's opinion but agree with other parts. People's opinions are not always clear-cut and can vary in terms of shade (or intensity). This is a key feature of reasoned discussion.

Illustrate what you mean by having a large, cuddly teddy bear on your knee and then making comments about it. For example, *I have a large cuddly cat here* and holding up the teddy. Ask the class if they agree with this statement. Model the talk frame answer for them by showing the prompt cards that you made earlier, filling in the appropriate verbal response: *I agree that it is large and cuddly but I don't agree that it is a cat.*

Next, give the children a less clear-cut sentence such as *This teddy is well loved and cost very little money to buy.* This time encourage them to use the talk frame, backing up their opinions using *because...* For example, they might reply *I agree the bear is well loved because it is worn, but I don't agree it cost little money to buy because it looks expensive.*

Once the children have got the idea, tell them that now they are going to try it out in a 'real' situation about something they all have a view on. Ask the class to think about their views on whether there should be a drinks machine in school (or any other relevant school issue such as wearing school uniform). Give them time to think of three reasons why they are in favour or against a drinks machine. Ask them to keep these completely secret from each other.

Objectives

To enable children to:

- develop discussion and debating skills
- begin to realise that opinions are not always clear-cut.

Cross-curricular links

English

Qualifying or justifying opinions after listening to others' questions or accounts.

History

Asking and answering questions; recognising that the past is interpreted in different ways.

RE

Appreciating different people's views and values.

Seat the children in a circle and start the discussion. Ask a confident child to start by saying *I think there should/shouldn't be a drinks machine in school because* _______ *and* _______ *and*_______, giving their three reasons. The others will then have a chance to reply, in turn, using the talk frame used earlier of *I agree* _______ *because…* or *I don't agree* _______ *because…* stating their reasoning. You may want to model this until they gain confidence.

After three or four children have responded using the talk frame, list some of their comments showing the different opinions.

Conclusion

Return the children's attention to the learning focus of the session and ask them to observe how most of them *both* agreed and disagreed with the first child's for or against statements. Use the examples recorded to show how some children's opinions might generally agree but will differ in shades of intensity. Remind the children that opinions are not always clear-cut and that there can be grey areas in between; it may not be possible always to come to a conclusion. To illustrate the point, ask the children to start to graduate some of the recorded comments from most sure to least sure about having a drinks machine to show how even opinions that agree can vary in the strength of that agreement.

Now or later

- Repeat the activity using another subject that occurs within school life such as whether there should be a football-only area of the playground or whether school dinners should be scrapped.
- Encourage the whole school to have such debates (meaningful ones with an outcome that will be acted upon) in assembly.

Viewfinder

Objectives

To enable children to:
- develop research skills
- learn how to access the most important information from a text.

Cross-curricular links

English
Scanning and performing detailed reading to find information.

History
Selecting and recording information relevant to the focus of the enquiry.

Design and technology
Carrying out a practical task.

Resources and classroom organisation

You will need: pre-cut strips of card 4cm by 30cm (12 strips for each group of three children); butterfly clips (12 for each group of three children); rulers; scissors and pencils; a variety of texts (the texts could be linked to a topic being studied in class; some of them should be text-heavy); a middle-sized viewfinder that is already made up (see instructions and diagrams in Figure 1); the instructions and diagrams from Figure 1 displayed on an OHP.

Introduction

Citizenship requires us to be able to access and evaluate information from a variety of sources. This activity literally puts text under a microscope. It develops the skill of narrowing down the focus to access specific information and gain the most useful parts of any information we are presented with.

What to do

Tell the children that they are going to learn how to be good researchers. Explain that a researcher is someone who finds things out. Hold up a challenging text (one with long, complex sentences, smaller print and dense text layout with few pictures). Ask the children why it is hard to get information out of this text.

Next tell them that they are going to create an information viewfinder to make researching information in a text easier. Show them the viewfinder you made earlier and demonstrate putting it over a part of the text to show how different parts of the text can be put into focus. Explain that they will be making three different sizes of viewfinder to suit different research needs. Ask the children to get into groups of three. Each group will make a set of three viewfinders. Demonstrate to the class how to make a viewfinder, and then put the instructions in Figure 1 on an OHP and give out the materials.

To make the viewfinder:

1. Mark the card strips at 5cm intervals:

2. Take two card strips:

3. Add two laterals:

4. Secure the strips with the butterfly clips:

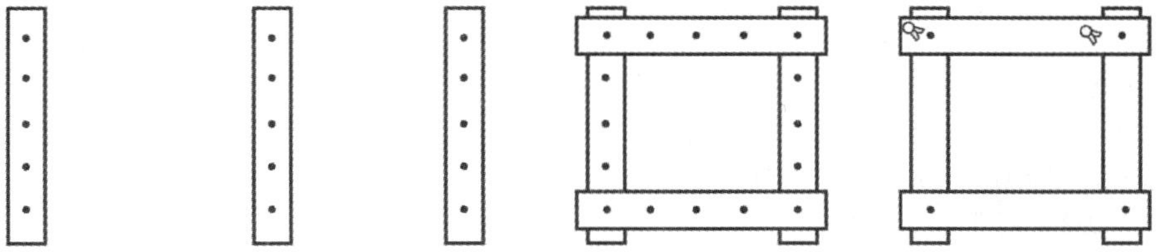

Each viewfinder is made in the same way. The only difference is where the cross-pieces are pinned to the lateral pieces. This creates the different size of view:

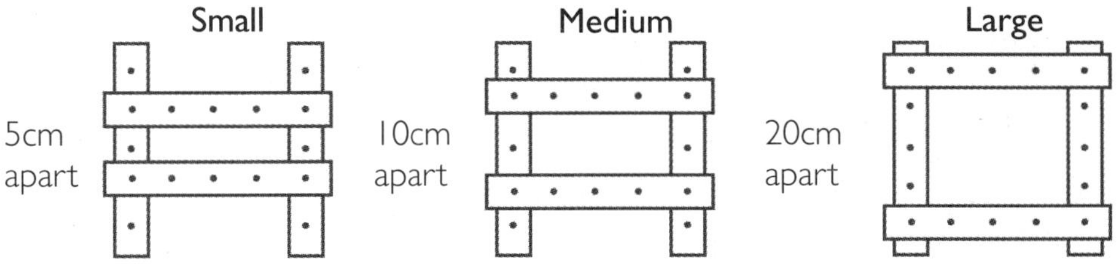

Figure 1

When the children have completed their viewfinders, ask them to come together while you demonstrate how the different sizes can be used. Choose a text and lay the large viewfinder on a random part of the page. Read with the children this part of the text. Ask them to discuss in pairs what it is about, then ask for feedback as a whole class. Ask them to choose a part of the text within the viewfinder that seems most important and that they want to concentrate on further. Next, demonstrate using the small viewfinder so that perhaps two sentences or even a single word that they chose to concentrate on are visible. Show how by first looking at a large piece of text (skimming) and then choosing to narrow the focus and looking at a smaller amount of text we can find the detail in a piece of writing.

Finally, use the large viewfinder again. Point out the advantages of being able to see what comes before and after the detail (it provides context). Explain to the children that the detail should only be considered when we have understood the wider context. Discuss with the children how using the three sizes of viewfinder can help at different stages of their information finding. For example, when they begin to research a project or topic it is often best to use the large viewfinder and then to spend more time reading the finer points that are relevant to their project. The small viewfinder can also be used to remove any information that they don't need.

Give the children a selection of texts to research from and let them experiment with the viewfinders.

Conclusion

When the children have had time to experiment, bring the class back together for a final discussion. How did focusing in different ways on the text help them to draw information out of it? When did they find the large viewfinder most useful? When is it good to have a larger view of the information? When is it useful to just focus on the small detail?

Now or later

- Start to focus the learning either by providing a set of questions for which the children need to find answers or giving pairs of children a general area of research to concentrate on.
- Use the viewfinders to focus on other contexts such as details of pictures, diagrams, fiction texts or text on computer screens.

Implications game

Objectives
To enable children to:
- explore the implications of a piece of information
- learn to develop critical opinions about information.

Cross-curricular links
English
Using inference and deduction, and looking for meaning beyond the literal.

History
Looking at implications of historical events.

Resources and classroom organisation
You will need: flip chart or board; paper and writing materials.

Introduction
In order to discuss and debate, we need to be able to evaluate and have a critical opinion about information. This activity helps children to understand the concept of *implication* in the context of a game, and the importance of evaluating the information they receive.

What to do
Explain to the children that they are going to be playing the implication game. The aim of the game is to get as many ideas as they can out of one piece of information. Model to the children what you mean by writing the following sentence on the board and illustrating it with a simple stick-person picture: *The man stood waiting at the station.*

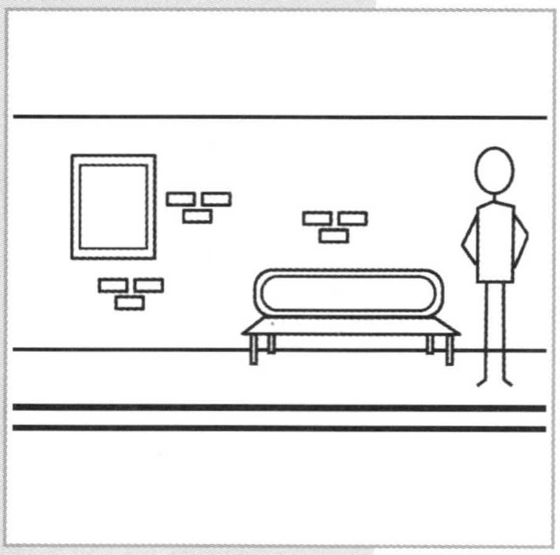

Make a list of all the children's suggestions of unseen things that could be true about this statement. For example, even though we don't see the railway track we can be almost certain there is one there. The information tells us this even though it doesn't actually say so in words or pictures. Explain that their suggestions are *implications*. Explain to the children how one small sentence implies many things. It implies that trains come in and out of the station, and that the man understands and knows that trains stop at the station.

To help children understand this difficult concept draw small sketches within clouds around the main sentence and picture to show the unsaid things that the sentence implies. Once the children understand the idea, ask if they are ready to start playing the game.

Write another sentence on the board such as, *The donkey moved slowly carrying a huge load* or *'Do you know this loaf of bread cost 99p?' said Mr Smith in a shocked voice.* In small groups, ask the children to write down all the implications they can think of relating to the sentence. However, explain to them that they will have to give a valid, sensible reason why they think the sentence implies what they've recorded. Any sentences that don't have a valid reason will be removed and the winner will be the group with the most acceptable implications.

After ten minutes, ask the groups to come together bringing their list of implications with them. Compare the number of sentences by asking each group to read out their work. Choose a few of the sentences, asking the relevant groups to give valid reasons for why they can state each idea. Explain that this is called justifying and that being able to justify what you say is very important if you want others to value your opinion. Encourage the children to challenge other groups and explain that they can learn to judge other people's opinions by deciding if the implications are justifiable or not.

Tally up the final list of implication sentences. The group that has the most is the winner. Congratulate the group.

Conclusion
Learning to imply possibilities of a situation can be useful. Can the class think of how it could help them when reading a complex story, or going to a new place that they have never been to before, or when researching a piece of information? (For example, signs to an airport and a railway station imply that a town is big with many facilities.)

Remind the children that it is important not to just accept information without questioning what it really means. (For example, the signs to the airport and railway station imply a large town, but the airport could be a private airfield and the railway station might be for freight only.)

Now or later

■ Set your class the challenge of making one implication for each different piece of information they receive that afternoon. Even such statements as *Put down your pencils* or *Tidy up* can have the same treatment given to them!

■ Use this new skill on a familiar piece of text, headline or information. Try working on a sporting headline such as 'Ginola to move to Milan'.

The CHECK test

Objective

To enable children to:

■ begin to evaluate the reliability of information.

Cross-curricular links

English

Distinguishing between fact and opinion; comparing information and persuasive texts.

Science

Analysing data.

History

Recognising that the past is interpreted in different ways.

Resources and classroom organisation

You will need: the CHECK test written on an acetate or flip chart (see Figure 2); two different types of information text, for example a page from a reference book about animals and an advertisement (one with plenty of persuasive devices and pictures) displayed on an OHP or make copies for the class to share; strips of paper or Post-it Notes to cover up parts of the text; a selection of different texts, for example sport scores, advertisements, fact sheets, recipes, instruction booklets, letters, diary extracts, reference books and so on.

Introduction

Everyone receives huge amounts of different information from a variety of sources: a key part of being a citizen is being able to decide how reliable that information is.

What to do

Explain to the children that they are going to evaluate some information to see how reliable it is. Can any of them provide a definition of *reliable*? Explain that reliable means how much you can trust and that to learn how to do this, they are going to use a single test that can be applied to all information that they receive – the CHECK test.

Now start the lesson by presenting the two texts (see Resources). Show the children how advertisements often use persuasive language, backed by glossy pictures and opinion-based statements written in a way that implies that they are fact. Compare this with how reference texts are impersonal and factual with no opinion. Diagrams and clear labelling might be present in this type of text too.

Ask the children: *How do we know if we can trust what we read in each text?* Allow them to suggest possible ideas then introduce the CHECK test, displayed on the OHP. Cover up all but the first letter (C) with a blank sheet of paper. As you introduce each step to the children, go through each of the explanations given overleaf, relating them to the two sample texts.

The CHECK test

Could it be fact or opinion?

How is it presented?

Emphasis?

Can we check it?

Kick out the rubbish!

Figure 2

■ Could it be fact or opinion? Remind the children of the differences between fact and opinion and give examples from the text. Show them how an opinion can sometimes be taken as fact, such as *It is a beautiful beach.*

■ How is it presented? Does the advert have a photograph of the product it is trying to sell? How realistic/reliable do the children think the photograph is?

■ Where is the emphasis? When information is written either in large letters or bold, it gives the impression that it is important. Are there any examples of this in this text? If so, do they match up to what should be the most important piece of information? (For instance, a large FREE headline in an advert could apply to free postage but the more important information telling you that a minimum order of £5 is required might be in small print at the bottom of the page.) Once we are aware of these possible pitfalls we can become more discerning in our judgement.

■ Can we check it? This is a vital skill and may be a hard concept for the children to grasp. Discuss with the children if there is a way of finding out this information from another source, for example you could look in an encyclopaedia to check facts about an animal. Checking the source of the information (who wrote it) can also be useful for checking reliability.

■ Kick out the rubbish. Having applied the previous four tests, go through and 'kick out' any information that is not reliable. This can be done by covering this 'disallowed' information with strips of paper or Post-it Notes.

Now review together the information that has passed the CHECK test in the two examples. Put this reliable information up as display to show how the process works.

Finally, give pairs or small groups of children a selection of different texts (see Resources), to run the test on.

Conclusion

Ask the children which of the texts they have looked at would pass the CHECK test and which that they think would fail. Remind them that they can carry out the CHECK test at any time and on any piece of information. It does not even have to be written down – they could do it in their head whilst sitting on the bus looking at an advertisement. Ask them to try it out on what people say as well, for example on television.

Finally, discuss with the children *why* it is important to check information for reliability. (For example, so you can know whether to believe what you are being told and whether the information is safe to use or act upon.)

Now or later

■ Children could apply the CHECK test to Internet texts. Do the same criteria apply? How could they check the source of the information, for example?
■ Continue collecting examples and set a challenge (could be a homework task) to see who can find the most misleading information example.

Section 2 DIVERSITY AND COMMUNITY

Identifying, respecting and celebrating differences and similarities is what makes all kinds of communities able to function well. This section focuses on exploring and celebrating individuals, communities and diverse ways of living.

WEAVING OUR LIVES TOGETHER

OBJECTIVES

To enable children to:
- understand that a community is made up of many different individuals
- appreciate that people's differences contribute to a rich community.

CROSS-CURRICULAR LINKS

ART AND DESIGN
Using a variety of methods to communicate observations, ideas and feelings.

RESOURCES AND CLASSROOM ORGANISATION

You will need: two pieces of A4 cartridge paper; coloured felt-tipped pens and/or crayons; collage materials; scissors for each child.

INTRODUCTION

Citizenship is dependent on the communities in which we live appreciating the strength that comes from the differences and rich variety between all members of the community.

Children need to feel that whilst there are many qualities that make us similar to each other, it is the differences we all have that make our class, school, street and community unique. This activity provides a practical exercise in which the differences are literally woven together to make something greater than lots of individual strands.

WHAT TO DO

Tell the children that in this activity they are going to think about how special and different they all are from each other. Go round the class saying one thing that you admire about each child, emphasising the different things so that no child has the same thing said about them. (For example, perseverance, helpfulness, strength, lovely smile, humour, interesting stories, good ideas.)

Tell the children that they are going to make a glorious multi-coloured carpet from all the special things about themselves. To create their part of the carpet, they will make their own personal design incorporating three or four key features about themselves. These could be anything they want such as birthday dates, signatures, favourite colours, names or pictures of favourite places and hobbies. Tell them that their designs will cover two sheets of A4 paper each. One piece will form the main structure of a carpet; the other will be cut into the strips to weave into the carpet. Give out the paper to each child and ask them to start the design. Ask them also to add one thing that they like about themselves or that they are good at. Emphasise that the greater the variety the more interesting and more colourful the carpet will be.

Use whatever art skill you or the children enjoy doing most to form the background patterns and colours. Each child could use the same types of colours and patterns so that their own identity is clear. They could also use computer clip art or drawing programmes to do this.

To create the carpets: use one piece of each child's decorated A4 paper, and fold it in half. Show the children how to cut from the middle fold to 4cm away from the edge. Repeat this process making ten cuts that are 1–2cm apart. This will form the border and warp threads.

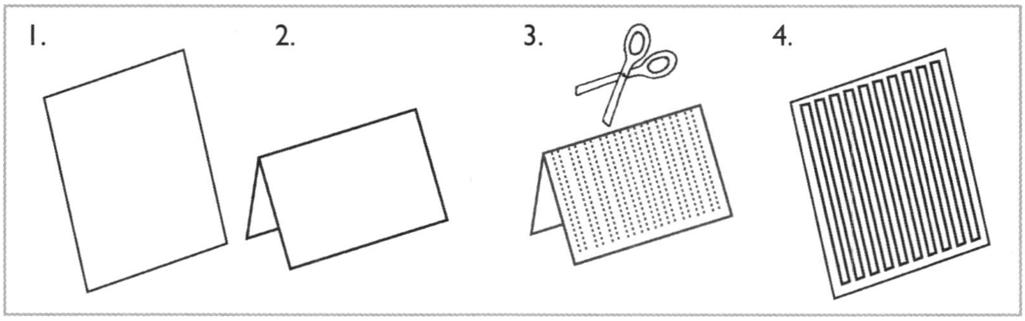

Using the other A4 sheet, show the children how to place it in portrait position and cut it into ten separate horizontal strips 1–2cm wide. Place all these strips into a class pot. Give out a random selection of ten strips to each child (or do a lucky dip) so that each child gets a collection of other children's strips. They should then weave these personal strips into the warp structure of the A4 frame that they have already created.

Conclusion

Discuss with the children how the mats represent the class community. Draw attention to how the rich variety of designs within the mat reflects the variety in the class. Ask the children: *What do the mats show us about our class? Look how colourful our mats are when we put everyone's special pictures and signs together, just as when we put all our different experiences and skills together we get a rich and exciting community.*

Now or later

- You could ask the children if they want to bring in things that are special to them to weave into their patterns. A ribbon from a special dress, wrapping paper from their favourite birthday present, even tickets to football matches or pantomimes could be stick to a strip and woven into the pattern.
- As a longer-term project, ask parents to contribute one thing that they would like to see woven into the community pattern.

Celebration pot

Objectives

To enable children to:

- recognise their own skills and qualities
- develop these skills and qualities.

Cross-curricular links

English

Make contributions relevant to a topic.

Resources and classroom organisation

You will need: a special pot or container (the 'celebration pot') wrapped in several layers of paper; strips of paper about 5cm x 20cm (one for each child); writing and drawing materials.

Introduction

Appreciating other people's strengths is a key skill of citizenship. Equally important, but often more difficult, is the skill of appreciating our own skills and how we can use them to greater effect.

What to do

Tell the children that today they are going to do something very special: they are going to fill up… Stop yourself mid-sentence and bring out the wrapped-up celebration pot. Without speaking, indicate to a chosen child that they should come forward and unwrap one layer. Then ask another child to reveal a second layer and so on until the celebration pot is revealed.

Explain that this pot is special because it can have the children's most special thoughts inside it. Today the children are going to fill it. They are going to think about the things they feel they are good at. It is very important at this stage that you give plenty of suggestions, otherwise they will just choose football or a school subject. Some possible suggestions include: playing with other children; having a good imagination; talking in a quiet voice; thinking up ideas; resolving an argument; running very fast and so on.

Ask the children to close their eyes and think quietly for 30 seconds. Then, ask them to open their eyes, turn to a partner (these could be friendship pairs) and tell them two things that they have thought of. Their partner should also add something that they think their friend is good at and vice versa. Next, give out a 5cm x 20cm strip of paper to each child. Tell them that these are celebration papers. Ask them to decide on one thing that they are going to write down or draw to show what they are good at. As the children finish, reassemble on the carpet and ask if any of them would mind you reading out what they have written.

Tell them that now they have identified one of their skills or qualities, they are going to plan how to use it to greater effect. Ask them to think about when they could use their special strength, and what it would be useful for. For example, talking in a quiet voice is useful when people are trying to concentrate, or when you want to make a quiet dramatic effect in a play.

Ask the children to think quietly again for 30 seconds. Then ask them to turn over their strip of paper and write or draw how they can make more use of their special skill. Now these celebration papers are ready to go in the celebration pot.

Make a ceremony of each child coming up to place their celebration paper in the pot. Each child could walk up and read out their celebration paper (if they are comfortable doing so), before placing it in the pot. When all the pieces of paper are in the pot, seal the lid so that all the special thoughts are safe.

Conclusion

Remind the children of what they have put in the celebration pot – their own special strengths – and how they are going to use them in many different ways. Ask the children where they would like the pot placed so that they can all see it. Tell them that whenever they look at the pot, they can think of all the ways in which they are good at things and how they can use these special skills or qualities.

Now or later

- Use the celebration pot as a way of extending the children's appreciation of each other by asking them if they would like to put special thoughts about people other than themselves in it. Read these out once a week.
- As the term progresses and the children develop and acquire new skills, repeat the celebration by asking the children to look back and realise how many other things they have become good at. Again, try and maintain a breadth of choice so that the children's horizons of what they could be good at are widened.
- The celebration pot idea could also be used as a worry pot. Children can go through a similar process, having first identified anything that they are worried about. In this case the pot looks after the worry so that the child can put it out of their mind until they want to deal with it. Often by that time the worry has solved itself.

Hidden history

Objectives

To enable children to:
- realise the diversity of our history
- realise that Britain has drawn from a mixture of many different cultures
- think about the lives of people living in other times and with different values and customs.

Cross-curricular links

History

Understanding that the past can be represented in different ways.

Resources and classroom organisation

You will need: a set of cards made from photocopiable page 18 for each group of four children and a set displayed on an OHP.

There is a whole-class introduction to the activity then the children play the game in groups of four.

Introduction

Everyone likes to feel that they belong. History is often used to celebrate heritage, but can be done in such a way that it sometimes disguises and leaves, or makes invisible, a lot of contributions that many different cultural groups have made over the centuries. This activity presents some of this hidden history in the form of a game and should act as a platform for the children to research lots more hidden history.

What to do

Introduce the activity as a history lesson with a difference. Tell the children they are going to play cards and that they are going to find out some information that even their parents or carers probably won't know! Talk over the concept of time passing and, referring to a timeline, remind the children of the different centuries (both AD and BC) and how we read the dates in history. Make links to a topic they have already covered in history to help.

Ask the children to get into groups of four. The winner in each group will be the child who can remember the most information on the set of cards. On each card is the name of an object or invention familiar to the children and underneath six categories with the headings: *Origin*, *Date*, *Expense*, *Importance* and *Interesting fact*. Read out each card in turn or display each card on the OHP, then distribute a set of cards to each group.

Appoint one 'dealer' in each group to spread out the cards face-down in the middle of the table. Player 1, the child on the dealer's right, takes on the person sat to their right – Player 2. Player 1 chooses a category to question Player 2 on (for example, *Origin*) and then randomly chooses a card. Player 1 has to ask Player 2 a question in that category from that card. If Player 2 answers the question correctly, they get to keep the card. If Player 2 doesn't answer correctly, the questioner (Player 1, in this case) gets to keep the card.

It is now Player 2's turn, and the child on her right – Player 3 – will be questioned and so on round the group until all the cards have been used up. The winner will be the player with the most cards.

When each group has used up all the cards, bring the class back together. Ask them what they have found out that they didn't know before. Which was the most unusual card? Which was their favourite card? Why? Now ask the children if there are any interesting, little known, or unusual facts in their families or communities that they could find out more about. Discuss what makes an interesting history fact and what makes a fact rather than a story (something that is true and checkable).

Conclusion

Ask the children why they think the facts that they have discovered today are not so commonly known. It could be that the fact that the majority of people couldn't write up to about 1900 means that only the history of richer and educated people reached history books. The history of people who had a low status in society such as servants or people from other cultures is also often left out. Ask the children to think about why it is important that people's history is not hidden from them (or not allowed to be forgotten). (Because they only get a select view of history if they're not told everything and it does not represent the contribution to our lives that different cultures have made.)

Now or later

- Try out different variations of the game, for example pairs of children place a set of cards face down on the table and play pelmanism. They take it in turns to try and turn up pairs. Pairs can be made by dates, ethnic groups and so on.
- Have an inter-group memory quiz. Each group takes it in turn to ask the next group in the circle a question about the cards. Encourage the class to make up their own rules.
- Create a class set of cards that relate to exciting and little-known history about the class or the area. This needs to be handled sensitively – only use information that the children volunteer and are proud of.

Appendix

- *A multicultural guide to children's books, 0–16+*, edited by Rosemary Stones has an extensive list of non-fiction books including the history of different cultures and groups. Published jointly by the University of Reading's Reading & Language Information Centre and Books for Keeps.
- *Black and British* by David Bygott (Oxford University Press). Looks at the history of the Afro-Caribbean community in the United Kingdom in an accessible style for older KS2 children.
- *Romanichal Gypsies* by Thomas Acton and David Gallant (Hodder Wayland). Part of the *Threatened Cultures* series; describes the Romanichal culture and explains why their way of life is under threat.
- *The History of Asian Communities in Britain* by Rozina Visram (Hodder Wayland). Part of the *History of the Communities in Britain* series.
- The Channel 4 Black and Asian History Map at www.channel4.com/blackhistorymap contains many links to websites about black and Asian history across the British Isles; a useful reference resource for adults.

'Take a seat, please...'

Resources and classroom organisation

You will need: flip chart or board.

At some point the tables and chairs will need to be arranged in the way they would be for an interview. Explain to the children that this varies in different circumstances. If possible, the interview role-play could take place in another room.

Introduction

This activity is designed to encourage the children to think more carefully about the jobs that people do in school and the different roles that people have in all sorts of organisations. The children should learn that all these people work together for the greater good of the whole organisation.

What to do

Ask the children how many different people work in the school, and what their jobs are. What are their job titles and do they know exactly what these people do? Write down their suggestions on a flip chart. List any other people who don't work in the school building but work for the good of the school and the children – school crossing patrols, for example. Prompt the children by asking: *Are there people who*

Objectives

To enable children to:

- recognise there are a range of jobs carried out by people in school and elsewhere, and the contribution these jobs make to each particular community
- learn which skills they can develop to make their own contribution in the future.

Cross-curricular links

English

Listening and responding to others appropriately; speaking with confidence for a range of purposes and audiences; taking part in role-play.

work in the school who you don't normally see? Are there other members of staff who your parents/carers might see? Explain that all these people have different roles and the school needs all sorts of skills, abilities and experiences to make it work.

After drawing up a list of the different roles, as a whole class talk about the qualities and skills that are needed to carry these out and list these on the flip chart. You can then introduce the main activity. Explain that the children are going to perform a role-play, where they will interview each other for different jobs within the school. Discuss together the sort of questions they think they should ask. For example, should they ask the same questions when they are interviewing for the posts of caretaker, cook, headteacher or PE co-ordinator? Ask the children to choose which post they would like to apply for.

The children should then work in small groups to interview for different posts. It would probably be sensible to interview for five or six different jobs, with an interview panel of three, and two or three children being interviewed for each post. Explain that before the interviews start, the interview panel has five minutes to work out which questions to ask, and who should ask them. Explain that the children should focus on what things they think will be needed for the particular job. During this five minutes, the candidates should work out some ideas about what to say in the interview. They can give themselves the skills they think they will need for that particular job.

After the interview role-plays, bring the children back to the carpet and explore how they felt when they were being interviewer and interviewee. Which candidates were most suitable, and why? Why would it be better to give the job of caretaker to someone who had basic skills in woodwork and plumbing, rather than someone who knew lots about computers? Can they think of the sort of skills they might need in order to apply for jobs in the future? How would they go about achieving those skills? Discuss how the sort of subjects they decide to take at secondary school might affect the sort of job they later apply for.

Conclusion

Explain that all skills are important to a community: a school, for example, cannot function properly if the people who work there do not have many different skills. Some of these skills could be useful in other situations. Where might a caretaker be able to get a job – which other large buildings might need looking after in a similar way? By taking an interest in lots of activities at a young age, children can decide which ones suit them, which ones they enjoy, and which ones they are skilled at. Moreover, it gives them an opportunity to identify the skills they would like to develop to give them a chance to work in an area in the future.

Now or later

- You might wish to hold mock interviews with people who already work in the school – or with people on the governing body who may work elsewhere.
- Video the interview process, and invite the participants to comment – how would they do things differently next time?

Familiar families?

Resources and classroom organisation

You will need: flip chart or board, large sections of used frieze paper, jumbo markers.

There needs to be space to display the large sections of frieze paper. Alternatively, these sheets could be put on tables.

Introduction

It is essential (though often difficult) to respect the family backgrounds and circumstances of all the children in your class. In many classes, there will be a large range of family groups. An activity such as this obviously needs sensitive handling, and children should never feel pressured to join in, or to talk about the details of their own family set-up. Children who do volunteer information should not feel that they are in any way being judged.

What to do

Ask the children what they think a family is. *What sorts of people are in a family? Are all families the same?* If the children do not readily come up with suggestions of a variety of family models, point out to them that there are a number of possibilities. We should be aware of these possibilities, and should not automatically think of married parents and children from that marriage. Write down the suggestions of people who could make up a family (these do not have to be real-life examples). An example could be a father, dad's girlfriend, a half-brother or a grandparent. Make it clear to the children that they do not have to talk about their family – they can talk about other families they know, or even families they have seen in films, on television or in books. A useful prompt here could be the novels of Jacqueline Wilson, which often involve a variety of family groupings. Accept all suggestions in this brainstorming activity.

Now explain to the children that they are going to choose five or six of the *fictional* suggestions they made earlier to make up a family. They could, for example, choose Dave, Dave's girlfriend, Granny Shaw, and the little brother, Pat. Put the children into five or six groups and allocate one family member to each group. They must discuss the family member – what they look like, how they walk, talk, what their name is and what sort of personality they have. They should draw this person life-sized and write the other information round the outside of the figure. After a suitable amount of time, when all the children have drawn their figures and written some labels and details on the frieze paper, ask the children to sit down and introduce their family member to the rest of the class.

Conclusion

The children can then discuss and decide what the relationships are between these different family members – how well they get on, and so on. Talk about how the children have challenged stereotypes in inventing this family group. Explain that a stereotype is something that always gets shown in the same way. For example, teenagers are usually shown with baseball caps on back-to-front, grandmas are usually shown knitting, and so on. In reality, there are lots of different teenagers, and lots of different grandmas. A stereotypical family is mum, dad and their two children. By coming up with a different family group, the children have challenged this stereotype, and given themselves the chance to think about different sorts of families. It will also have helped raise the children's own feelings of self-esteem towards their families.

Now or later

There are clear links between this activity and the 'Family bingo' activity in the companion Key Stage 1 book. That activity could be used as a follow-up with younger Key Stage 2 children.

Objectives

To enable children to:

- be aware of different types of relationships
- recognise and challenge stereotypes
- feel positive about themselves and their families.

Cross-curricular links

Art

Recording from experience and imagination, and to make thoughtful observations about starting points and ideas in their work.

Name Date

Hidden history

THE NUMBER SYSTEM: 1, 2, 3...
Origin: the Hindus, India.
Date: 5th century AD; introduced into Europe around AD1300.
Expense: no cost.
Importance: extremely.
Interesting fact: it is traditionally believed that the Arabs invented our current method of writing numbers, but in fact they simply passed it on to European culture from the Hindus.

CHOCOLATE
Origin: discovered in Mexico.
Date: bought to Europe by Spanish explorers in the 1500s.
Expense: at first very expensive and only wealthy people could afford it, now very cheap.
Importance: chocoholics would say vital!
Interesting fact: when chocolate was first imported it could become poisonous if it went mouldy.

THE CALENDAR (365 DAYS/12 MONTHS IN A YEAR)
Origin: Ancient Egyptians.
Date: 3000–2000BC.
Expense: none.
Importance: very, especially for calculating birthdays.
Interesting fact: the Romans complicated things for a while because of their superstition that even numbers were unlucky – their months were either 29 or 31 days long.

POTATO
Origin: native to South America.
Date: introduced to Western Europe by Spanish explorers in the 16th century.
Expense: cheap.
Importance: a primary food in Western diets.
Interesting fact: poteen is a strong alcoholic drink made from distilling potatoes.

FIREWORKS
Origin: Ancient Greeks and Romans.
Date: AD670.
Expense: from £3 to £1000s.
Importance: highly enjoyable but not essential.
Interesting fact: first called 'Greek Fire' and used as a weapon before guns were invented.

PYJAMAS
Origin: originally worn as loose trousers in hot countries such as Turkey, India and Eastern countries.
Date: introduced to England in the 17th century and adopted there as nightwear.
Expense: anything from £4 to £100s.
Importance: fairly useful.
Interesting fact: pyjama comes from the Persian word *pājējāmah* which means 'leg clothing'.

ALPHABETS
Origin: the Western alphabet is based on one developed by the Phoenicians, a seagoing people, who lived on the shores of the eastern Mediterranean.
Date: 1500BC.
Expense: none.
Importance: vital for the development of literate civilisations.
Interesting fact: earlier alphabets were based on pictures; the Egyptians used hieroglyphics from 3000BC.

VIOLIN
Origin: Arabic culture.
Date: began to be used in Europe in the 13th century.
Expense: from £30 to millions for a Stradivarius.
Importance: culturally very important for Renaissance and classical music.
Interesting fact: the violin developed from the Arab instrument, the *rebec*.

LOLLIPOP
Origin: Romany (gypsy).
Date: over 200 years ago.
Expense: cheap.
Importance: enjoyable but not essential.
Interesting fact: in Romany *lolli* means 'red' and *pobbel* means 'apple'. Toffee apples used to be called *cosh-lollipop* (*cosh* means 'a stick').

PAPER
Origin: China.
Date: believed to have been discovered in AD105.
Expense: quite cheap.
Importance: vital for the development of literate civilisations.
Interesting fact: in Ancient China paper that was written on was sacred: all waste paper was gathered up and burnt, and ashes flung into the sea as offerings to the God of Literature.

UMBRELLA
Origin: China, Ancient Egypt and Rome as parasols to shade people from the sun.
Date: brought to Western Europe in the 17th century where they were used to shelter people from rain.
Expense: £2 to £1,000s.
Importance: extremely useful for people living in wet climates.
Interesting fact: *umbra* is the Latin word for 'shade'.

CHRISTMAS TREE
Origin: decorating a pine tree for Christmas is a German custom, introduced to England by Prince Albert, Queen Victoria's husband.
Date: German origins date back to medieval times; in England from the 1840s.
Expense: more expensive in southern countries where they have to be imported.
Importance: an important tradition for many Christians.
Interesting fact: in Brazil Christmas occurs in summer and people decorate pine trees with pieces of cotton to represent snow.

Section 3 ENVIRONMENT

Developing a sense of responsibility is a crucial area of citizenship education – responsibility not only to ourselves and other people, but also to the natural and built environment. Indeed, the citizenship guidelines require children to learn how to make more confident and informed choices about the environment. The activities in this section provide the knowledge, understanding and motivation that children need in order to accept this responsibility, and to see it in a positive and constructive light.

THE PLEDGE TREE

RESOURCES AND CLASSROOM ORGANISATION

You will need: various pieces of green paper (gummed, sugar, frieze, and so on); a bare tree (no leaves) drawn on a large sheet of frieze paper; scissors; glue; pens; jumbo markers.

Children can make the leaves on their own after whole-class discussion on the carpet or at tables. It is important that the children are seated in such a way that they are creating a pledge for themselves, and not writing the same as their neighbours.

INTRODUCTION

The activity serves as a starting point for children thinking about the environment. They should all be encouraged to make simple pledges, but there should be no suggestion of compulsion. As with all activities of this nature, nothing will be gained by coercion, which goes against the whole ethos of citizenship education.

WHAT TO DO

Ask the children what they understand by the word *environment*, writing their suggestions on a flip chart, and try to reach a consensus. Talk briefly about some examples (local and global) of damage we do to the environment. You could mention litter in the streets near the school, throwing away things that could be recycled, cutting down ancient forests or using cars too much. It may be possible to link an example to some work you are doing on a particular topic, such as electricity, the rainforest.

Ask the children if they, or other people they know, do anything that might help to limit the damage we do to the environment. They might suggest using energy-saving light bulbs, recycling newspapers, bottles and cans, or riding a bike for short journeys. Help the children with more simple suggestions if they find this difficult.

Tell the children that they are going to make a pledge tree about the environment. At this point you may need to explain what a pledge is. You can say that it is a promise to yourself or to others that has to be carried out; what you promise to do will be seen and heard by others, so it is very important to keep

OBJECTIVES

To enable children to:

- make responsible choices, and take action
- recognise that their actions can have an effect on the environment.

CROSS-CURRICULAR LINKS

GEOGRAPHY

Recognising how we can protect the environment and seeking to manage environments sustainably.

ART

Exploring a range of starting points for practical work; working on their own and collaborating with others on projects in two and three dimensions and on different scales.

it. Obviously, the activity only makes sense if the pledges are kept, so there must be a degree of honesty and realism. Possible pledges include: *When my mum and dad go to the supermarket I will take the old newspapers to recycle. I will turn the television off properly at the end of the night, rather than leaving it on stand-by.* Write the children's suggestions down on the flip chart.

Explain that the children are going to draw leaves on the green paper, then write their pledges on the leaves, cut them out and stick them on the tree. Point out the tree drawing on the frieze paper at this point. Show them an example of a leaf, which should be about 10cm long. Write your own pledge on this leaf. If there is a classroom assistant or other adult in the class, they should also do this. The children should then go to their tables to make their leaves and write their pledges.

Bring all the children together and ask them to read their pledges out and then stick the leaves on the tree. It is vital that the children do this themselves. This is their pledge tree, and ownership is very important. As they stick their leaf to the tree tell them they should sign the trunk of the tree, and that this commits them to the pledge they have made. Display the tree prominently.

Conclusion

Ask the children if they have made responsible choices, and what inspired them to make those particular choices. Explain that even the smallest of changes can make a difference to the environment, and that if they stick to the actions they have pledged, they will set an excellent example for others to follow. If adults see young children being responsible, it will help and encourage the adults to be more responsible, and to think about what they are doing.

Now or later

- The children could make a 'home' pledge and a 'school' pledge – one would be a promise to do something environmentally friendly at school, and the other would be a promise to do something similar at home.
- In assembly, on a regular basis, children can volunteer to say how they have kept their pledges.
- Some children might want to create new leaves for themselves. Parents and other people from the wider school community could add leaves. This could evolve into a design and technology project to accommodate all the leaves. The next step could be to make another tree, a small group of trees and so on. The initial tree should be of a size that can be covered quite quickly so that the children can visibly see the progress. It is possible to use fallen branches for a more prominent and permanent 3-D display.

Traffic calmer

Resources and classroom organisation

You will need: flip chart or board; an enlarged copy or OHT of photocopiable page 26 plus enough enlarged copies for one between each group of two to four children; coloured pencils; scissors; card for each group of children.

Introduction

Citizenship requires our involvement in our community. One of the most immediate areas of concern to children and adults is road safety and the balance between planning for safety and keeping the roads as workable routes for moving vehicles. In this activity the children are put in the position of traffic/road planners. The activity involves breaking down the problem before choosing some solutions. It is important to remember that the key skill here is not getting a right answer but being able to justify clearly why the chosen solution is the preferred one.

What to do

Introduce the activity by displaying photocopiable page 26 on an OHP. You might choose to be in role as a councillor who is instructing the city planners. If you do this direct the class to their seats as they enter and start the lesson fairly formally, introducing yourself and welcoming them to the 'Emergency planning' meeting. Explain to the class that the street map shows an area where there is a problem about the safety of pedestrians due to the speed and volume of traffic.

First the planners need to identify areas of danger for both road users and pedestrians. Ask the class to get into working groups of two to four children and give out the street maps. When the groups have looked at the maps, ask the children to work out where they feel the danger areas to be for the different groups of users. Ask them to mark these danger spots on the map. They can colour code to show which category of user is in danger. Some of the dangers that might be identified could be: school exit where children could run out onto the road; parents picking up from school causing congestion; the park exits where children could run out; allotment tenants arriving, leaving, needing to unload equipment or supplies; the hospital which requires a fast road for the accident and emergency entrance in contrast to the school which should have a slow moving zone round it; lorries making deliveries to the factory. The children may come up with many different possibilities. Make it clear that there is no right or wrong answer(s), however the group must be able to give a well thought-out reason or justification for their view.

After ten minutes ask the planners to reconvene with their maps to discuss, briefly, some danger areas that they might have identified. Emphasise that everyone will have a different selection of danger points. List all the danger points the class gives you on a flip chart.

Either in role or as yourself, ask the planners what sort of strategies could be used to overcome the dangers. There will be many suggestions: pelican or zebra crossings, traffic lights, crossing patrols, railings or gates, road narrowing, speed bumps, a one-way system and no-entry signs, pedestrianising an area, a toll system to let cars in, speed cameras. Use your judgement as to how much input you want to give in addition to the children's suggestions.

Following this 'briefing' send the groups back to work to plan in the safety features of their choice on their street maps. They can do this by drawing counters to place on the map, or drawing features that can be made into stand-up models that can be placed on the street plan.

Objectives

To enable children to:

- break down problems and consider solutions
- realise that they can choose to change our environment
- understand that modifying an environment can involve difficult decisions
- learn how to justify their opinions.

Cross-curricular links

English

Making contributions in a group – justifying opinions, and presenting information to different audiences.

Geography

Learning about how making decisions about places and environments can affect the future quality of people's lives.

Emphasise that they must discuss each traffic-calming strategy carefully in their groups so that they can justify it later during a presentation but that otherwise, whatever they decide to put in place is their choice.

Conclusion

When you feel the groups are ready, ask them to present their maps and solutions to the whole class (or council meeting). The class should check that all the ideas are justifiable ones. Ask the children if they found the solutions to the problems difficult to make. Were there any conflicting interests of the different road users? Point out how it is important that they realise they can change (or councils/governments can change) their environment for the better and safer.

Now or later

■ You could make this presentation as formal as you wish. It might be a separate lesson to which other people are invited (the school crossing patrol, headteacher, local safety officer or community police officer). You could provide the groups with OHTs so that they can summarise their reasons for the different solutions.

■ Arrange a class visit to the council planner's office.

■ Research your local area. Map the street surrounding the school and assess the safety issues and need for any traffic calming.

■ Compile a questionnaire for local people to assess their views both of traffic safety in the area and their requirements as road users.

Fuel bill mystery

Objectives

To enable children to:

■ discuss the effect the school has on the environment

■ be able to make real choices and justify an opinion.

Cross-curricular links

English

Qualifying and justifying opinions.

Science

Thinking creatively to try to establish links between causes and effects.

Geography

Understanding how a school's environmental impact can be reduced.

Resources and classroom organisation

You will need: enough sets of the cards from photocopiable page 27 for each group of children.

The activity can work when children are in pairs or small groups. It is important to organise the groups so that all children are able to contribute ideas and participate in the discussion.

Introduction

A 'mystery' is a way for children to tackle a given question or problem. Discussing the problem will help with many thinking skills, such as information processing, reasoning, enquiry, evaluation and creative thinking. It is important that children know *how*, as well as *what* to learn. One of the most important points to stress to the children when doing such an activity is that there is no right or wrong answer – the discussion and justification of their viewpoint is the important thing.

What to do

Explain to the whole class that they have to answer one simple question using the information provided on the cards: *Will the school succeed in reducing its fuel bills?* Make sure that this question is displayed prominently and that the children have their own copy of it. It is important to stress to the children that there is no right or wrong answer. The important part of this activity is the discussion, and being able to justify their reasons for coming to a particular point of view or conclusion. Explain that fuel bills refer to the amount of money that the school spends on gas, electricity, oil and so on, to heat, light and generally keep the school running. Ask the children briefly if they can think why it might be good to reduce the use of these resources.

Put the children into pairs or small groups and give each grouping a set of the cards from photocopiable page 27. Tell the children that these may help them answer the question. They have to decide how relevant or important the statements on the cards are. They might sort the cards into different groups – things that would reduce the fuel bills, things that would increase them, things that would have no bearing and red herrings (you will probably need to explain this term). Emphasise again that there is no right or wrong answer – you want to hear the children in discussion. The children should then go to their tables to think through the problem. Try to ensure they are seated in such a way that they will not be influenced by the opinions of others nearby.

Bring the children back together, and ask them to say whether they think the school will succeed in reducing its fuel bills and, most importantly, *why*. Children from all the groups should be introduced into this concluding discussion, and everyone must have the opportunity to air their views.

Conclusion

The success criterion for the activity is whether all the children have spoken, and justified their opinion.

Return to talking about the question itself – who would benefit if the school did reduce its fuel bills? Would this be a matter of the school saving a few pounds, or could there be other benefits? Discuss the environmental implications of heavy resource usage, focusing on the issues raised in the mystery cards.

Now or later

- Have a go at making your own mystery. It is recommended that there should be between twelve and twenty statements.
- Older KS2 children could use it as a project – they could attempt to make mysteries for their classmates or younger children.

Transport chaos

Objectives

To enable children to:

- realise the need for balance in the environment
- understand how cars damage the environment.

Cross-curricular links

Science

The cycle of respiration in the atmosphere.

Geography

Looking after the environment.

Resources and classroom organisation

You will need: a supply of red and green beanbags (enough for two for each child in the class); a large storage box big enough for all the beanbags to go into (the balance box); two benches.

A hall or the playground is probably best for this activity, as the children need a large area to run around in.

Introduction

Everyone recognises the need to protect and have respect for the environment, but often the issues are hard to understand. This activity teaches a major environmental issue through a practical game. It is intended as a starting point both for children's environmental knowledge and their understanding that they themselves have a direct impact on the environment.

What to do

Tell the class that today they are going to learn about the greenhouse effect. Ask if any of them know what this is before demonstrating how it works.

Split the class into two halves and ask one half to stand up. Tell them they are going to pretend to be trees! Trees are special because they give out oxygen. Give them each a green beanbag and explain that this represents the oxygen. Then ask the other half of the class to stand and tell them that they are humans, who need oxygen to live. Then explain the other part of the story, that the trees need to take in carbon dioxide to be able to live and this is what the humans are breathing out. Give the humans a red beanbag each – this represents the carbon dioxide. Then ask each tree to form a pair with a human and exchange beanbags with each other, to demonstrate the giving and receiving of oxygen and carbon dioxide. Make sure the children understand that everything is well balanced at this point.

Explain to the children that the carbon dioxide (CO_2) is useful because it takes in the warmth of the sun and heats up the earth. If this did not happen the earth would be one enormous ice sheet, and humans and most animals and plants would not survive.

Throw a red beanbag to a child and ask them if they are getting warm (because the CO_2 absorbs the warmth of the sun and warms us up). Do this a few times to different children repeating the same question. Then throw a lot of beanbags (very carefully) at one child. Ask them if they are really hot now. Use this to explain how too much CO_2 heats up the earth too much and that we need to have a good balance of green and red beanbags (O_2 and CO_2) to keep the earth from heating up too much.

Then tell the children that they are going to play a game where they will try to unbalance the levels of O_2 and CO_2. Ask the class to stand up and form their groups again, giving the trees two green beanbags each and the humans two red beanbags. Introduce the balance box and tell both groups that they are going to run one by one to the balance box and put in their beanbags. As they put their beanbags in they can take out two beanbags of the opposite colour and return them to their 'base' (a bench set aside at one end of the hall). Each child can then collect two of their own coloured bags from their base again and repeat the exercise. No one is allowed to hoard bags and no touching of the opposite side is allowed!

Start the game and after three minutes of frenetic activity tell the children to stop. Sit the class down and count the number of green and red beanbags in the balance box. The balance ought to be fairly even. Remind them what the beanbags represent and point out that the balance of O_2 and CO_2 in the world means a temperature that is just right for us.

Now tell the class that you are going to introduce the motor car to the game to see what happens to the balance box. Take three children from each group and tell the class that these six children are now cars. Explain that when petrol is used in cars it causes CO_2 to be released. Allocate an area where the petrol is kept and place two red beanbags per car in that area (make sure the children realise why they are red). Tell the class that the cars will collect their petrol and run and put their beanbags into the balance box in the same way as the humans and the trees. Stand up the trees and the humans and deal out the green and red beanbags as before, and now with the three groups start the game again.

After three minutes stop the game again and count the beanbags in the balance box with the class. This time the balance should have been tipped towards red bags. Run the game again when the green team will be working even harder! When the balance is counted it will *still* be towards the red bags.

Conclusion

Whilst the children cool down ask them why they think the reds have won and what difference the introduction of the car made. Ask them if they can tell you what the increase of red beanbags means. Some children will, but remind the others about the increase in temperature it causes. Tell them that this is what is called the greenhouse effect.

Explain that it is called this because our world becomes like the inside of a greenhouse – the heat comes in but it can't get out. If the temperature gets too hot it will affect the whole world. Ask the children if they can think what the effects of this around the world would be (the polar icecaps will melt and some countries will be flooded; animals will no longer be able to live in environments that have changed). Ask them how they think we could make the balance between red and green equal again. See if they suggest increasing the green players and realise that planting more trees does indeed help reduce the temperature by producing more O_2.

Now or later

- Play the game again, but increase the number of trees by including a group of tree planters.
- Make a class display showing the things the children have learned whilst playing the game.

Appendix

- Greenpeace at www.greenpeace.org provides excellent information posters.
- Try Friends of the Earth at www.foe.co.uk

Name Date

Traffic calmer

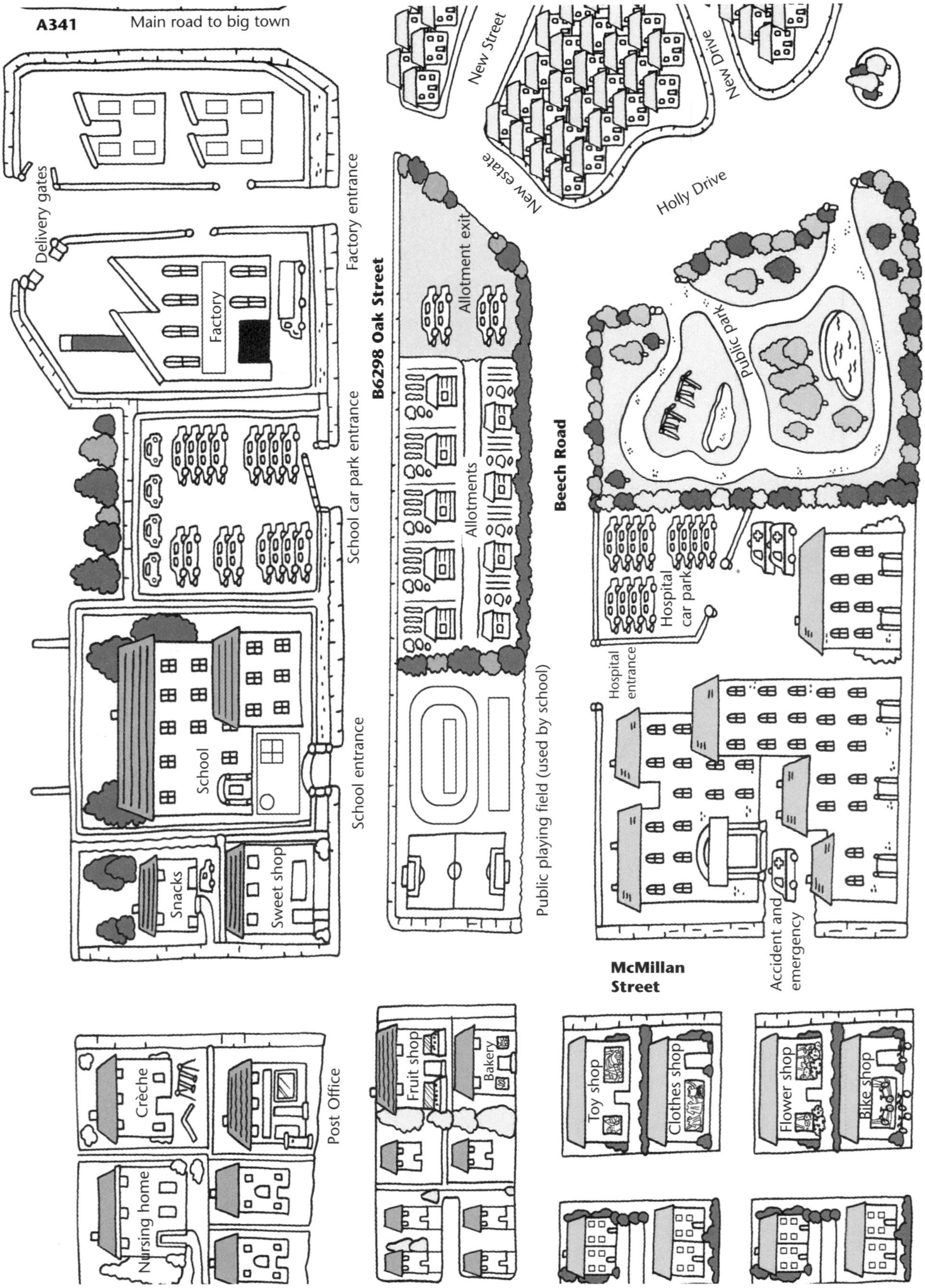

Name Date

Fuel bill mystery

The Headteacher limits the amount of photocopying.

The caretaker draughtproofs the doors and windows.

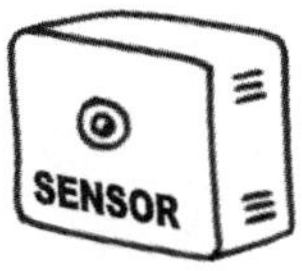

Sensors are fitted to rooms, switching off lights when the rooms are not in use.

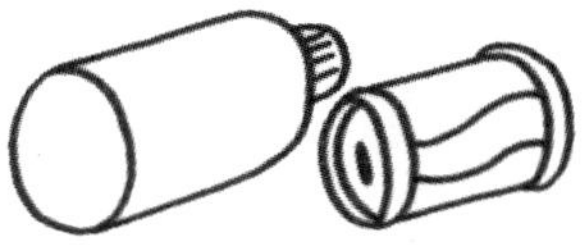

The children recycle plastic bottles and aluminium cans.

The caretaker installs new windows which open in two different ways.

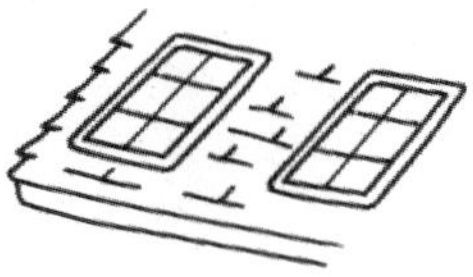

Solar panels are fitted to the roof of the school building.

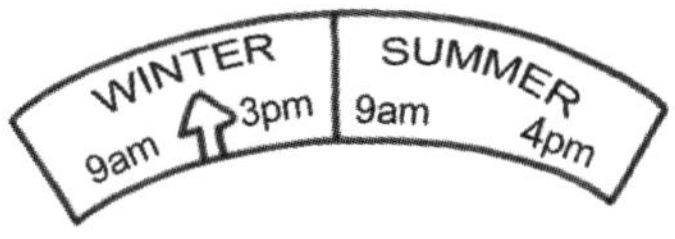

The school day is shortened in the winter, and lengthened in the summer.

The radiators are painted blue.

The school has a Green Team who encourage everybody to 'think green'.

A gas fire replaces the electric fire in the staff room.

The school sets up a walking bus, where children walk accompanied to school.

Staff have a 'cycle to work' day.

Energy-saving light bulbs are fitted in all the offices.

School dinners are cooked elsewhere, then brought to school in vans.

Water butts are bought to collect rain water.

Preparing to play an active role as citizens is one of the key features of the guidelines for citizenship at Key Stage 2. At this age, it is important that children take a greater interest in the world around them. Contributing to the school community and to communities outside school is an essential part of developing citizenship skills. Children must learn that their decisions and actions can have an effect on local, national and global issues. They should begin to foster an awareness of the democratic process, which they will study in more detail at Key Stages 3 and 4.

ACTION STATIONS

OBJECTIVES

To enable children to:

- recognise the role of local and national government
- recognise the role of voluntary, community and pressure groups.

CROSS-CURRICULAR LINKS

ENGLISH

Listening and responding to others.

MATHS

Recording information in diagrammatic form.

RESOURCES AND CLASSROOM ORGANISATION

You will need: the 'stations' written on large sheets of sugar paper or frieze paper and a set of question cards (see 'What to do').

This activity would ideally be suited to a hall, gym or other large room where there is space for the children to safely run about. You may want to consider the footwear, clothing and jewellery the children are wearing.

INTRODUCTION

The activity is designed to be a fun introduction to thinking about politics and democracy. Many young children have little understanding of who is responsible for a number of decisions and events in their everyday lives, and this activity encourages them to think about such issues, and also directly instructs them in certain areas, such as which organisations are responsible for running healthcare. The important point, as with many activities in the book, is that the children are engaged in thought and discussion. There is no need to talk too much about words and phrases such as politics, democracy and government, though it is important that the children begin to grasp some of the differences between certain basic institutions and groups.

WHAT TO DO

Explain to the children that they are going to play a game similar to one they may know as 'Stations'. Tell them that in this version they will run to a station which they believe gives an answer to a question the teacher poses. Emphasise that they will not be penalised for making a wrong answer or guess.

It is suggested that the stations are: local government/the council; national or central government; charities/voluntary bodies and you (the children themselves). The children must have some understanding of the terms used on the stations, so some discussion around these must take place first. It will be helpful to give examples of some of the things the various bodies do. It must, however, be remembered that the children are being taught about this during the activity, and some of this teaching will be relatively didactic.

You should take on the role of question master, a role that can be played to the extent with which you feel comfortable.

Write questions to ask the children on brightly coloured cards, perhaps with a question mark on the back (the side visible to the children). Some sample questions are: *Who decides how much teachers get paid? Who pays teachers? Who organises research into cancer? Who pays for the bins to be collected? Whose job is it to make sure the paths in front of our houses are kept clean? Who makes sure the sea is not polluted? Who is responsible for the welfare of farm animals? Who is responsible for making sure that we keep fit and healthy? Who pays Jobseekers Allowance? Who pays for the police? Who pays for closed circuit TV in town centres?* Rather than give too long a list of such questions here, it is probably better if you use some of these suggestions, and choose some others with which you feel comfortable. Make the whole activity as much like a game show as possible. It is intended to be fun!

When you have read a question, the children must run to the station that they think gives the answer. You must then say which station is correct. In some situations there may be more than one correct answer (such as when voluntary and statutory bodies fund research into a health issue). Some questions should be open to interpretation, such as *Who is responsible for making sure young children do not smoke?* Possible answers to such a question could be the children themselves, parents/carers, teachers, the national government or voluntary bodies. As with many of the activities, it is important you do not present yourself as the font of all knowledge. After some explanation, and discussion with the whole class, ask the next question, and so on.

Conclusion

Bring all the children back together. You may want to do this back in the classroom. Ask them to discuss what they have learned. Are they now clearer about the different roles of the different bodies? The activity should raise just as many questions as it answers. You may wish to repeat the activity, and make a record of the answers – the correct stations – this could be in the form of a simple grid. It might also be possible to use Venn or Carroll diagrams to show the information.

Now or later

- The game can be used as part of a full discrete lesson about citizenship, or as a short filler, where only a few questions are asked.
- The children can make their own version of the game. They could come up with different questions for the same stations, or they could come up with their own stations and accompanying questions.
- Invite local councillors in to school. Explain the game and what you have found out. If there are any particular gaps in the children's knowledge or any misconceptions about the role of certain bodies, ask the councillors to clarify. An extension of this could involve asking members of the council, community bodies, voluntary organisations and pressure groups, along with your local MP.

Soapbox corner

Objectives
To enable children to:
- explain their views on issues that affect themselves and society
- discuss and debate topical issues.

Cross-curricular links
English
Speaking with confidence, and gaining and maintaining the interest of different audiences.

Drama
Evaluating how they and others have contributed to the effectiveness of performances.

Resources and classroom organisation
You will need: six wooden boxes or stage blocks for the children to stand safely on. (These can be optional, but one of general description should certainly be used for the final part of the activity.)

Groups should contain a mix of both children who are likely to speak in front of others and those more reluctant, and also those with an interest and enthusiasm for topical issues and those who have other interests. A clear space is very useful, so it may be appropriate to clear tables and chairs to the side of the classroom, or alternatively use the school hall or other clear communal space.

Introduction
The purpose of this activity is as a starting point for children to explore topical issues. It is designed to be fun, and is the sort of activity where children are not conscious of the fact that they are doing any sort of 'work'. You must make sure that the children maintain this enthusiasm, while also sticking to the objectives outlined above.

Some children will find the prospect of going on the soapbox particularly daunting, so they must be accommodated. Probably the best way of doing this is to make sure that the children realise that they are allowed to speak from the floor in a more anonymous way.

What to do
Explain to the children that they are going to be discussing a topical issue. Explain that this is something in the news which people all over the country or local area are talking about. Also explain that people have different views on the matter, but it is important that everybody gets a chance to air their views.

Ask the children if they know what a 'soapbox' is. Show them the box or boxes you are going to use to stand on. Talk about how there are certain places, such as Speaker's Corner in Hyde Park, London, where people get on a soapbox and talk about something which matters to them, or about which they have a strong opinion.

Now ask the children to think of a topical issue they feel strongly about. If the children cannot think of anything, then use an issue that regularly comes to the public's attention, such as whether or not to ban foxhunting. Find six children who are willing to speak on the issue. (Ideally, these six children should hold differing opinions and/or arguments on the issue.) These six children should now each be put into a different group with the other children and they should practise talking about the views they hold regarding the issue – if they do not hold firm views, they must try to put themselves in role. This first session is almost a rehearsal, and the other children in the group should come up with questions and comments from the floor to enliven the debate. At this stage they should be helping each other within the group and encouraging debate and ideas.

Now bring the children back to the carpet. Explain that the children in each group who have been listening and commentating are going to go around and listen to the other speakers who will stand on soapboxes, if you have some available. Each speaker now has to try to convince a different group of children of their argument and point of view. You should circulate and listen to all the speakers at some point. If you feel particular children are running out of things to say, think of questions to help. This is also a role that other members of the class might be able to take on.

To finish, one or two particularly eloquent speakers (ideally, a girl and a boy) should get the chance to air their views in front of the whole class on the soapbox. The rest of the class should be free to respond as appropriate.

Conclusion

Gather all the children together and ask them to discuss the arguments they have heard. Which speakers do the children think spoke well, and what were the reasons for this? What qualities do the children think are necessary for a good speaker? Is it important to be loud and clear, or to alter our voice when we are talking? What happens when we are loud or drop our voice at certain times? Suggest it might be a good idea to keep the message simple, and to repeat certain points. How did the speakers feel when they had the chance to stand on the soapbox to express their opinions? Did they find it easier or harder when there was input from the other children? How do the children (from both the listeners' and the speakers' perspectives) think the activity would alter if they had the chance to go away and do more research about a particular topic or issue?

Now or later

- The activity could be extended to include more research on a particular issue. Try different scenarios where the speaker or the audience is better informed. Is it obvious which side has researched the subject?
- Run the activity when there are local or national elections taking place. Children could stand as candidates for the main parties, and they can address the rest of the school from the soapbox during an assembly, or a series of assemblies. Brave teachers could try to have two or more soapboxes at the same time! At such times it is possible to invite candidates from the political parties in to speak – most of them would grab the chance to air their views.
- The soapbox can also be used to discuss topical issues during assembly on a more regular basis. It may also be possible to invite people who represent different views in to school to participate in the discussion.

Rights

Objective

To enable children to:

- to be aware of the rights that they and other children have.

Cross-curricular links

English
Writing captions.

History
Human rights.

Drama
Using mime to explore issues.

Art
Making posters to communicate ideas and observations.

Resources and classroom organisation

You will need: a camera (optional) or art materials and large sheets of paper for display.

A rehearsal and performing space. This might be a hall or gym but could equally well be the classroom.

Introduction

Children's rights are enshrined in the United Nations Convention on the Rights of the Child that was drawn up in 1989. The citizenship guidelines require that children realise that they have rights.

What to do

Begin by telling the children that in this lesson they will be learning about something called their rights. Explain that a right is something they are entitled to have, such as the right to have enough food.

Explain that children all over the world have these same rights, and the rights should be respected by everyone. Some of the rights may not seem to apply to the children, but it still important that they know them so they can be aware of what other children are entitled to.

Read out the rights from Figure 3 to the children. Now divide the class into working groups of three or four. Tell them that since many people, adults as well as children, are not aware of children's rights they are going to bring the rights to

UN Convention on the Rights of the Child 1989

1. The right to be treated equally – whatever your race, colour or country.
2. The right to grow up in good health.
3. The right to have a name and a country.
4. The right to have enough food, a house and care if you are ill.
5. The right to have special care, if you have special needs.
6. The right to love, understanding and care.
7. The right to go to school and have a chance to play.
8. The right to help straight away if there are disasters.
9. The right to be protected from cruelty.
10. The right to grow up in a peaceful and loving world.

Figure 3

everyone's attention. They are going to make up a two-minute scene, mime or tableau that shows a right in action. This scene will then act as the basis either for a poster or photograph display. Give each group a right to work with and tell them that they should first discuss the right and what it means. After five minutes, let them move to a rehearsal space. Tell the groups that they have 15 minutes to sort out their scenarios.

During this time go round to each group, asking them: *What are you wanting to show? How are you doing that? Will you use words or mime? Does everyone need to move?* (This last question is to focus the attention on the staging of the scene. Often when children act or mime they feel the need to add lots of running on and off stage, forgetting that the words or actions do the movement for them. The most effective scenes will be where there are two or three small strong movements, nothing more.) At the end of the rehearsal time, bring the class back together and ask each group to show what they have done.

After all the groups have performed their scenes, ask the class for their feedback. Ask them: *What was the most effective way to convey the message? Which was the easiest right to recognise? Was this the easiest right to understand?* Which rights do the children think would be the easiest to implement? Which would be the hardest? Emphasise that there are no right and wrong answers here. Through this discussion, the class will become more familiar with the rights.

Conclusion

Finally, ask the groups to pick out a single frozen moment from their scenes that they think best represents their right. Either take photographs or get the children to record the images as pictures or posters to create a whole-class display. Ask each group to write a caption stating their right.

Now or later

Hold a 'Rights for all' assembly and perform the mimes.

Appendix

■ Save the Children produce (free) an excellent booklet specially designed for young people (also one for younger children), and also a teaching pack *Partner in Rights* giving a huge collection of creative activities. Tel 020 7703 5400 ext 2268 or www.savethechildren.org.uk

■ UNICEF also produce useful literature on the subject of children's rights.

You can save the world!

Resources and classroom organisation

You will need: flip chart or board.

Introduction

Both adults and children often feel frustrated by things that they would like to see done differently or completely changed. One of the key skills of citizenship is understanding the notion that we as citizens should, and can, be involved in changing and running our communities. This activity aims to show how frustration can be used to plan positive action to solve a problem to make change in our own communities. Planning action needs clear logical steps with plenty of time for discussion (including disagreement), reflection and evaluation. This activity aims to provide that structure so that it can be used with any problem that the class identifies.

What to do

Introduce the idea of a problem that frequently causes frustration in school. It could be anything from a boring playground, not enough room to play football, bullying, a desire for better school dinners. Agree on one problem to focus on, for example the boring school playground.

Tell the children that they are going to work out how to take action and find solutions for the problem. The strategy you are going to show them can be used for any problem. On the flip chart, list the six action points of the strategy:

1. Take an inventory.
2. Record the information.
3. Identify all the problems and possible solutions.
4. Reflect on and refine the list.
5. Research.
6. Create an action plan.

1. Take an inventory. This means assembling all the available information: existing facts, other people's views (positive and negative), your own thoughts, views of experts, possible sources of information, or talking to other people who have (or have had) the same problem.

To do this, divide the class into research teams with each team either taking responsibility for a different area of information, or asking a different year group, non-teaching staff or parents, their opinion. Information gathering could continue over a period of time.

2. When all the information has been gathered, each team reports back and all the information is recorded centrally. This could be done on the flip chart or on a computer. As the information is recorded, sort it into positive and negative categories, problems arising to be solved and possible solutions. For example, parents think the playground looks dirty and shabby and their solution is to 'brighten it up'. This would go into the positive list, one that offered a solution.

3. As a class, look at the information that has been recorded and decide on one or two main problems that need to be solved. For example, it could be that the playground contains loads of rubbish and has no structures to play on. Next, ask them to identify what action they need to take (get rid of the rubbish and get some structures to play on). Then identify any further actions they will need to take to achieve the above (for example, arrange for the rubbish to be taken away to the tip). You could set it out like this:

Objectives

To enable children to:

- break down problems and consider solutions
- draw up action plans
- recognise that people can become involved in how their communities are run.

Cross-curricular links

English

Planning and drafting information.

Maths

Presenting and interpreting solutions to problems.

	Main problem	How?	Action
What is wrong with our playground? →	lots of rubbish →	get rid of the rubbish →	arrange to be taken away to tip

4. Ask the class to consider everything they have collected so far. Tell them that this reflection time is important. As a class, agree on which courses of action you want to pursue and which you are going to leave. Then allocate areas of research to the groups. For example, for the playground: cost factors, safety issues, materials needed, funding, labour (who will build it?).

5. This is when the children find out how viable all the options are by researching (again in their groups). This might include getting information from the Internet, libraries, sending off for information, telephoning council departments, consulting experts (perhaps the caretaker, parents or other members of staff).

6. Finally create an action plan using all the information gathered, using small identified actions from the options they have researched.

Conclusion

Remind the children of where the project started: with their frustration at something they were not happy with. Point out how their careful analysis and planning have brought about an entire action plan for change. They have gone from complaining about something to taking positive action to improve it. This is what citizenship is all about: being involved in creating change for the better.

Emphasise the fact that the same steps could be used to plan any action in response to a problem that they have identified.

Now or later

- Carry out the action plan for real!
- Make a presentation to show other classes how the class has created this action plan.
- Widen the focus to a national or world problem and give the class the challenge of coming up with a action plan following the same steps.

Section 5 MAKING CHOICES AND RESOLVING DIFFERENCES

Citizenship involves the children recognising that they can make choices about many things, such as right and wrong, fair and unfair. It also helps them to see that often things can be more complicated than merely a clear-cut choice. It is vital to teach the skills of thinking, justifying and weighing up information, so that children can make choices based on what they know. It is also important that they learn to respect the different choices that other people make.

IT'S YOUR CHOICE!

RESOURCES AND CLASSROOM ORGANISATION
You will need: one enlarged copy of photocopiable page 42 and copies for each group of four children; two counters and a dice for each group; an OHP.

INTRODUCTION
A key feature of citizenship is that each of us is responsible for what we do and that we need to take responsibility for our actions. By realising that all our actions affect other people and things, decisions become more weighty and considered.

This activity aims to teach this realisation through a board game based on the traditional game of snakes and ladders.

WHAT TO DO
Introduce the concept of actions having consequences by demonstrating an example, such as up-ending the classroom bin and having to use a vacuum cleaner or dustpan and brush to clear up the mess, or shaking up a pop bottle before opening it! Ask the class what they notice about the actions you have carried out. Do all actions or decisions have messy or negative consequences? Ask them for some different examples of how our actions or decisions can have both positive and negative consequences. For example, if we decide to practise at something we will improve, if we forget to bring money to school we can't buy a ticket for the disco. Explain that they will play a game that explores how they have choices over their actions and that these actions often have consequences that affect themselves and other people.

OBJECTIVES
To enable children to:
- understand that they can make choices about their actions
- realise that their actions have consequences that affect themselves and other people.

CROSS-CURRICULAR LINKS
SCIENCE
Establishing links between cause and effect.

ICT
Exploring models to investigate and evaluate the effect of changing values.

Display photocopiable page 42 on the OHP. Choose three or four volunteers to be game demonstrators. Ask each of them to throw the dice in turn. The highest score starts the game (they can choose which starting place – A, B, C or D – to start from). The object of the game is to reach the centre point – 'You are a winner!'. Some squares have an instruction on where a decision has already been made for the children. The ladders are a result of a decision with positive consequences, whereas the consequences of some decisions will be negative and the player gets swallowed by a snake and emerges further back along the course. Explain to the children that whether they go up or down is based on luck here. However, there are intersections where players must make a choice. The routes are colour-coded so it is clear which route the intersection belongs to. These give the opportunity of crossing to a quicker route to the winning point if the right choice is made. The children should follow the direction of the arrow next to the decision they decide to make.

Split the class into groups of four, give out the boards and let the children play. When the class has tried out the game two or three times, assemble again on the carpet. Can

they see now how those actions that led to a ladder would have positive consequences? Do they understand why those decisions that led to snakes had negative consequences? Discuss how much of the game was based on luck and how much was about making the right decision. Talk about how the decisions made would have affected other people, not just themselves. For example, how would the person who lost their wallet be affected if it wasn't handed in to the police? What would be a consequence of saying a nice thing about a friend's work?

Conclusion

Are there any situations in life that are similar to those they experienced in the game, such as deciding whether or not to tell a teacher that someone is bullying your friend? What consequences have happened as a result of decisions they have made in their own lives? Ask them to think of and tell their talk partner about a decision they made in their own lives that brought about positive consequences. We can foresee the consequences of most of our actions. How do they think we can use this to help us to make smart decisions?

Now or later

Children can make their own board games based on the same format as the one in this activity. You might wish to base it round a specific subject such as the rainforest, bullying in school, or spending money. (The game could even have a historical perspective, for example the Tudor consequence game might include: living in the city means you might get the plague, going to court means you might say the wrong thing and get your head chopped off or you make influential friends and get rich!)

Thinking about feelings

Resources and classroom organisation

You will need: flip chart or board; three to four simple 2-D cut-out card puppets of boys and girls for each group of children; cards with different emotions (for example, happiness, jealousy) written on them.

The whole class should be seated on the carpet at the beginning. The children later work in groups of three to four. It is suggested that friendship groups might work well for this particular exercise.

Introduction

Through the safe, distanced medium of puppets, children will learn that how they react and respond will have an effect on others, as well as themselves. Children will be able to explore feelings and emotions using puppets, and in this way will learn to care about other people's feelings. The children will also learn that people express emotions in different ways, and that this is acceptable.

What to do

Begin the activity with a whole-class discussion about times when we might experience particular emotions or feelings. Discuss any events or occasions that have made you and the children feel happy, sad, angry or excited. Talk about such times in some detail, and begin to focus on each emotion in turn.

Next, together with the children, develop a simple storyboard on the flip chart showing a time when a child felt a particular emotion and the reasons for it. (Ideally a child should volunteer for their experience to be made into a storyboard and this should be sensitively handled. Alternatively, you may wish to use a fictional example.) Discuss how and if other people were involved and the effect the child's emotion had on these people.

The children should then be split into groups of three or four. The task for the groups is to go away and use the puppets to make a simple puppet show detailing the events in the storyboard you drew on the flip chart. Tell the children to use language to express the emotions at this stage, that is the puppet characters should speak. Give the children a specific time limit, say five minutes, based on your knowledge of their capabilities and their experience of this sort of work. Encourage them to try and keep it as brief as possible. One or two of the groups should then share their shows with the rest of the class.

The next task involves each of the groups being given a card with a different emotion to enact, using the puppets. Each group must clearly show the emotion being expressed and the reason for the emotion and also the effect it has on the other characters/puppets.

Finally, bring the children back together and ask each group to present their puppet shows to the rest of the class. The other children should try to work out which emotion is being expressed and why the character is feeling that way. Then ask them how the main character's emotion and the way they expressed it affected the other characters. Discuss why this is and (if any characters were hurt) how this could have been avoided. Ask the children: *Is it good for the character to be feeling that way, and to be showing how she feels?* Discuss this issue. If one of the shows focused on the emotion 'anger', you could ask the children if they thought it was right that the puppet character was being angry. Can the children think of another way the puppet character might have behaved? How did the other puppet characters respond to the anger?

Objectives

To enable children to:

- care about other people's feelings
- that their actions affect themselves and others
- to know when to voice their feelings.

Cross-curricular links

English

Using character to convey story, emotions and ideas.

Science

Exploring shadows with puppets.

Conclusion

Broaden the discussion as much as possible. *How often do we notice how our friends and family are feeling?* Discuss whether we always let people know how we are feeling, and what the consequences are if we do/do not.

Discuss with the children times when they may have bottled emotions up, only to regret it later, such as when they don't tell people they are upset, or when they are angry that someone is ignoring them but they don't tell them. Make sure the children know that there is another side to this coin – sometimes uncorking the bottle abruptly without thinking it through first can lead to problems. For example, we may get angry with the wrong people. Explain how this can hurt people's feelings and we should consider the impact it may have on others before we uncork the bottle.

Now or later

This activity can link well with work on anger management, particularly as it allows a safe distance from the intensity of the emotion itself, and could be used in a lunchtime or other extra-curricular club for children with behavioural concerns.

Roll the dice

Objectives

To enable children to:

- resolve differences by looking at alternatives, making decisions and explaining choices
- know where individuals can get help and support.

Cross-curricular links

English
Recalling and re-presenting important features of an argument or talk; making relevant contributions and taking turns; qualifying or justifying what they think after listening to others.

D&T
Making models.

Resources and classroom organisation

You will need: a copy of photocopiable page 43, scissors and glue for each group of three to four children. Children should have paper and writing materials to record some of their thoughts and feelings, and the points they discuss as they do the activity.

If you are carrying out this activity with younger Key Stage 2 children, you may wish to provide them with standard dice and write the situation and solution options on a piece of paper, rather than them making the dice themselves. The game essentially works the same way – if they roll a three, they refer to the third situation on the piece of paper, then roll again to find a possible solution – but with no need for cutting and sticking skills.

Introduction

This activity explores a number of situations, and possible solutions to these, that children may encounter during the course of a school day. The situations are relatively commonplace, or certainly within the imagination of the children. The children have to talk about the best way of dealing with each situation, and how they might make such a choice.

What to do

Tell the children that you are going to be discussing some of the sorts of incidents which sometimes happen in schools. They are incidents that need to be resolved, or sorted out – a decision must be made about what to do.

Give each group of three to four children a copy of photocopiable sheet 43. Demonstrate how to make the two dice, helping those children that need it. Explain to the children that they must roll die A to find out what the situation is. Die B should be rolled to find a possible solution to the situation or problem.

Emphasise to the children that they should discuss whether or not the solution rolled fits the situation on the first die. For example, would they say something straight away if they saw somebody writing on the toilet walls? Do they think it is a suitable solution? What other possible solutions could there be? The important point is that the children are discussing how appropriate a particular solution may or may not be each time. The children should also think about and discuss amongst themselves whom they can turn to in a particular situation.

Conclusion

Bring the class back together. Lead a whole-class discussion about some of the situations and their responses. Why did they think a particular solution was (un)suitable? Ask other children to comment on ideas and see if the speaker can then explain their choice of action to convince the other children. Ask if anyone else can suggest an alternative. Was there another avenue that could have been explored, for example was there somebody else they could have turned to in that situation?

Now or later

The children can write their own situations and solutions. They could devise a similar activity that they could share with other children in the school.

Making smart choices

Resources and classroom organisation

You will need: photocopiable page 44, paper and writing materials for each pair of children.

Introduction

A key skill of citizenship is to be able to make choices, some of which will be difficult. This activity teaches children some skills to make smart choices in general, but also has a specific focus relating to alcohol and cigarettes.

Making sensible choices about illegal substances is difficult. Children often feel that to appear cool or be part of the group they might experiment with drink or cigarettes without being aware of the dangers involved. It is an area that is often discussed with insufficient information to enable children to make choices. Opening out the discussion takes away the mystery of using such substances, and can enable the group to feel grown up by considering the information and then making their own choice. The session is about information, but if it is put back into the frame of 'it is naughty and teacher says you shouldn't' then many children may feel they have to show they won't listen to any 'boring old school advice'. This activity is designed to allow the children to start making their own choices based on reliable information.

When discussing any sensitive issues in the class it is important to work in partnership with parents and within the school's health education policy. Inform parents and carers that you are doing a lesson which involves using information

Objectives

To enable children to:

- realise that in order to make smart choices we need to use reliable information on which to base these choices
- be able to make smart choices independently without peer pressure.

Cross-curricular links

English

Researching information, selecting key points, and presenting this information; participating in discussion and debate.

PSHE/Science

The effects of tobacco, alcohol and other drugs on the human body, and how these relate to their personal health.

about alcohol and tobacco. Explain that the purpose is to help children make informed and sensible choices independent of peer pressure, using information from the NHS's National Drugs Helpline and The Health Development Agency – this will reassure them.

What to do

Seat the children in an adult way (chairs in a 'conference' circle). Welcome them to the young people's decision-making group, and tell them that they are going to learn the skill of making 'smart' choices and that today those choices are to be based on alcohol and cigarettes.

Explain to the children that when they are faced with difficult choices, they need to consider how reliable the information available is. Emphasise that first we need to know where the information has come from in order to evaluate if it is reliable. For example, information from someone who wanted to impress you is probably not reliable, or a piece of information qualified as 'what Tom says' needs to be checked out. Where did Tom get it? Information from an official organisation, which is checked by other bodies, will be reliable. Tell them that all the information they get today comes from government health education bodies. They make no money out of the information, and this may be another important factor when deciding if information is reliable.

Tell the children they are going to be put in pairs. Each person from each pair will go away and become an expert on a particular issue, before taking this expertise back to share with their partner. Divide the class into pairs and ask the children to number themselves 1 and 2. Now ask all the '1s' to form a group and all the '2s' another. Give copies of one information card from the photocopiable sheet to all members of the '1' group, then copies of the second information card to the '2' group.

Give each group a copy of the questions from the photocopiable sheet. Go through all the questions to check that everyone knows what they mean. Explain to the children that they need to weigh up the information on their card by asking these questions. Remind them that they know that the information on their card is reliable, and that later they will be able to use it to decide on the pros and cons of the different substances and make a decision for themselves, without being swayed by what their friends think (peer pressure).

Ask them in their number groups to make a list of the pros and cons, bringing in any other factors they want to. Tell them they should record the answers to the questions.

When the group have discussed their particular drug, ask the children to return to their pairs to present this information to their partner. The focus should be on presenting the information, but they can also offer some comment on any opinions that have been voiced. Ask each child to weigh up the pros and cons from all the information that they now have for both substances but make it clear that they won't be asked to give that opinion openly.

Give the pairs time to hear the information, then ask all the children to come back together. Remind the class that this session was about making smart choices based on reliable information. Did they feel they had enough information to weigh up the good and bad reasons for drinking alcohol or smoking cigarettes? Ask the children if they have learnt anything they didn't know before. Have they got any questions that they want to ask you?

At this point have a general class discussion about the different substances which they have discussed. (It is important that you speak with confidence and honesty in this part of the activity. Admit if there is anything about which you are unsure, making a point of telling the children that it is important that you too continue researching reliable sources of information on which you can base smart choices.) Would they know where to get reliable information about other drugs if they needed it? (The National Drugs Helpline offers confidential advice, see Appendix for contact details of this and other organisations.) Make it clear from what you say that drinking and smoking have real health risks which could and do endanger lives, quite apart from being illegal for children, whilst acknowledging also that many adults do drink and smoke.

Conclusion

Ask the children to discuss how they could use all this information if a group of friends (or bullies) was pressurising them to try drinking or smoking. How could they use this information to make a smart choice? Could they tell the person pressuring them about the health risks, while acknowledging the appeal? Would they be able to say that yes, alcohol would make them relax and have a laugh, but it would also damage their liver? Ask the children to consider how they have assessed information in order to make good decisions.

Do they now feel more able to make smart decisions independently without peer pressure?

Now or later

- Ask the children to think how, in their pairs, they could present this information to someone who knew nothing or very little about making decisions regarding the use of alcohol or tobacco. This could be in the form of cartoons, a leaflet, a rhyming poem or song, a television documentary.
- Design, write and illustrate two leaflets – one a generic 'Making smart choices' leaflet and the other specifically about 'Making smart choices about drugs'. Send the latter to the local Health Authority, and ask for a response. It may be that they would be able to use aspects of it in some of their future literature.

Appendix

- The National Drugs Helpline provides excellent leaflets aimed at different age ranges, suitable for both parents and children. Telephone 0800 776600 or visit the www.ndh.org.uk website.
- Alcohol Concern gives general information about alcohol misuse. Telephone 020 7928 7377 or visit the www.alcoholconcern.org.uk website.
- The Health Development Agency has a website specifically for teachers and children with links to other useful sites at: www.wiredforhealth.gov.uk

Name Date

It's your choice!

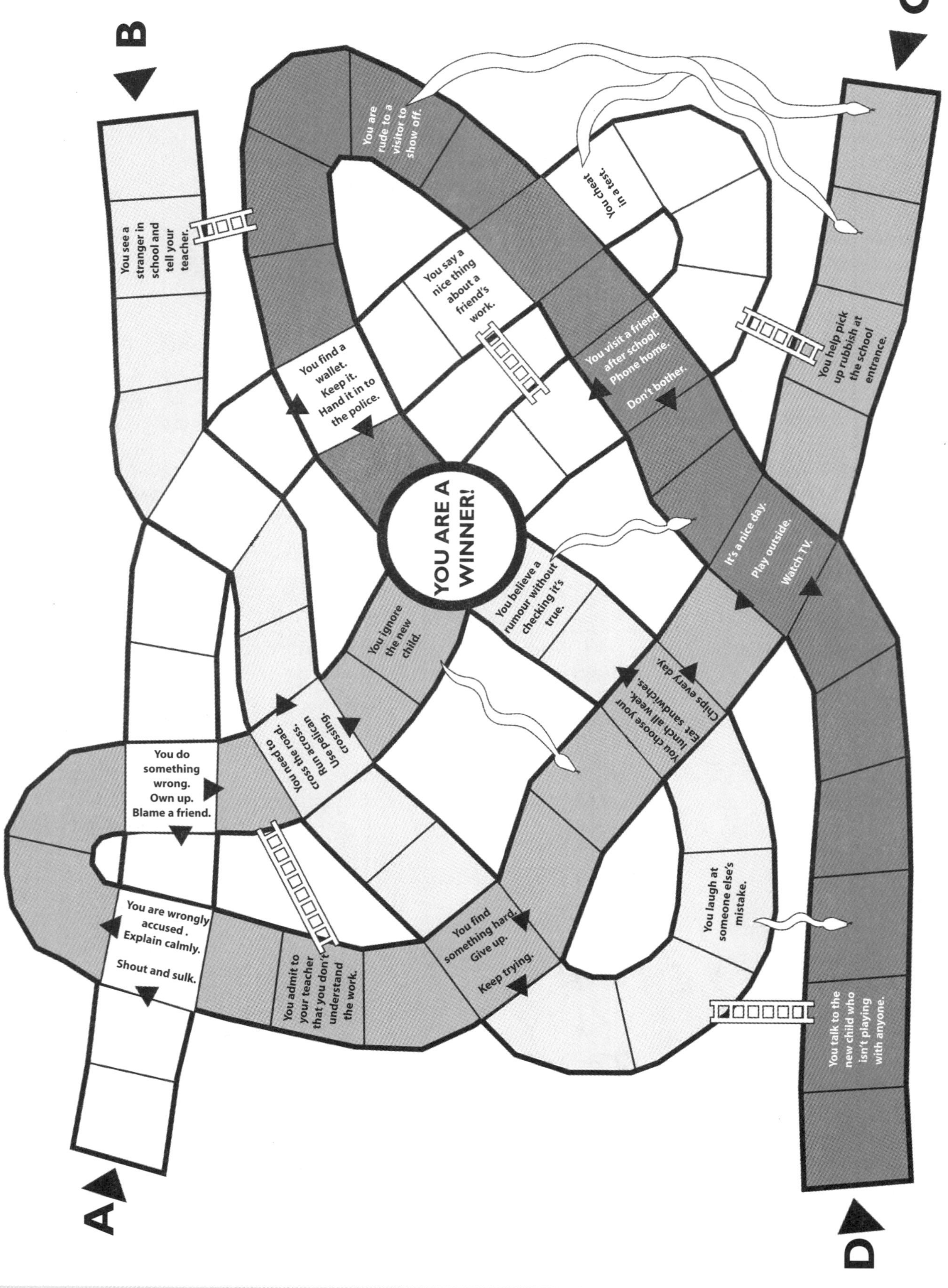

Name   Date

Roll the dice

Dice A

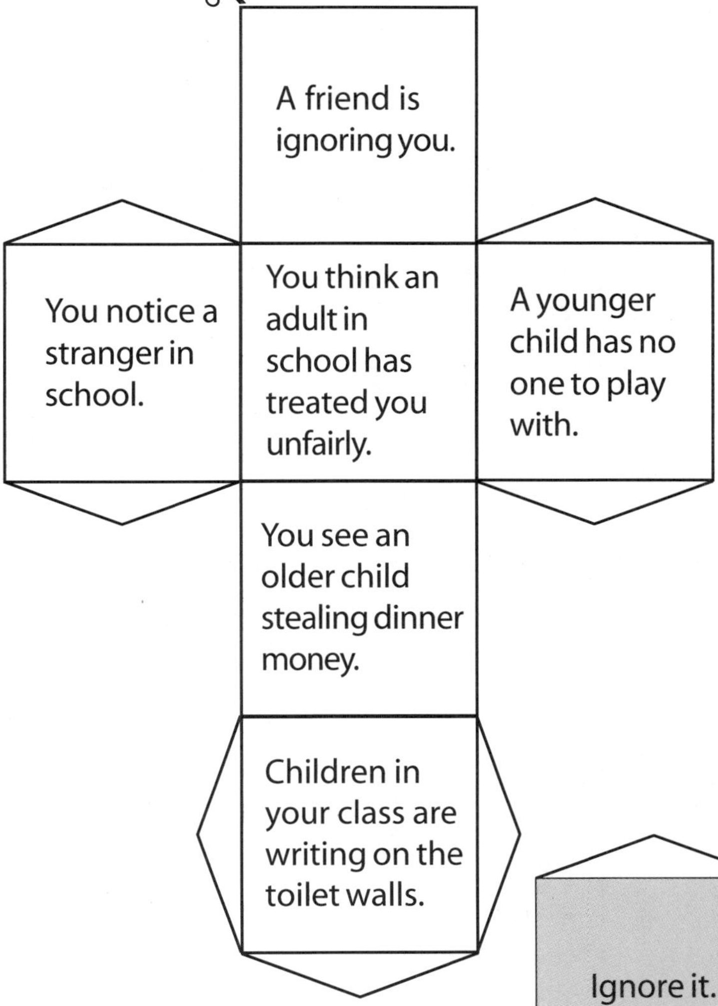

Dice B

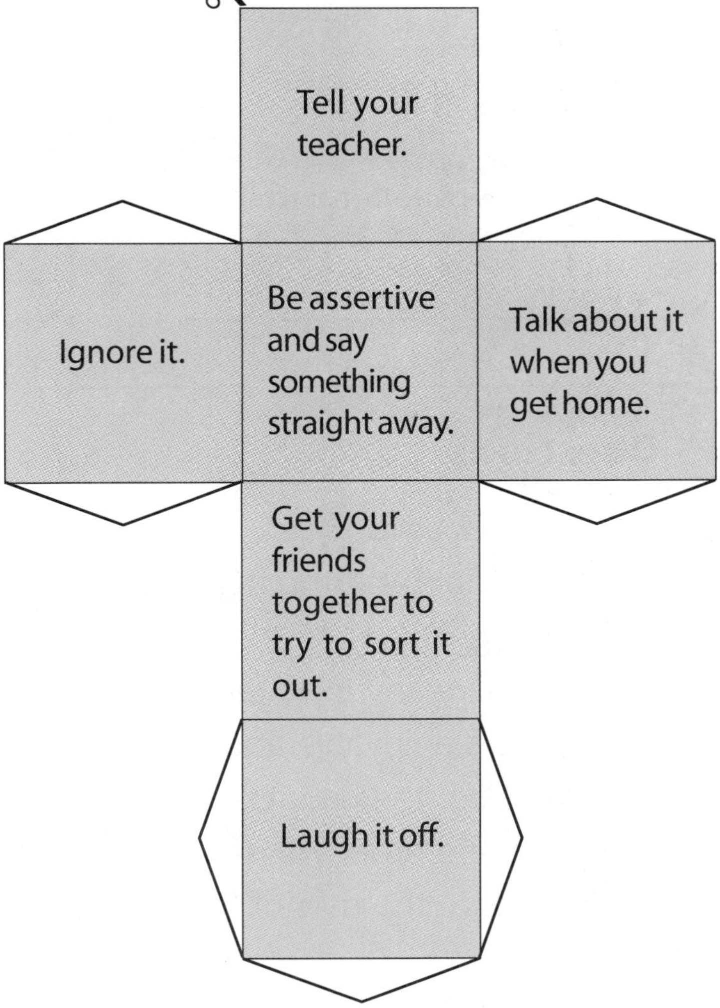

Name Date

Making smart choices

Alcohol

- It is illegal for under-18's to buy or be sold alcohol (except for 16- to 17- year-olds having a meal in a pub or restaurant).
- It can make you feel more relaxed and confident.
- People who regularly drink a lot of alcohol can become addicted.
- Alcohol can make you feel very sick and cause you to become clumsy.
- Small amounts can cause young people to be drunk quickly.
- Even one-off episodes of heavy drinking can damage your body.
- Half of pedestrians killed in road accidents have high alcohol levels in their blood.
- Regular drinking increases the risk of liver damage, cirrhosis and cancer.

Based on material supplied by the Health Development Agency and The National Drugs Helpline. © Crown Copyright. See www.wiredforhealth.gov.uk

Cigarettes

- It is illegal to sell tobacco to under-16s.
- Tobacco contains nicotine, which is a drug.
- Nicotine is a very addictive drug – once you start smoking it is very difficult to stop.
- Many adult smokers wish they never started – most smokers start in their school years.
- Smoking makes your breath smell and turns fingers and teeth yellow.
- Smoking can cause chest problems, cancers and heart disease.
- Some of the main reasons young people give for smoking include being sociable, appearing mature and fitting in with their friends.
- Smoking can kill.

Based on material supplied by the Health Development Agency and The National Drugs Helpline. © Crown Copyright. See www.wiredforhealth.gov.uk

Questions

- What does it do to my body?
- What does it do to my mind?
- Is it legal?
- Are there any long-term effects (good or bad)?
- What is enjoyable about it?
- What are the dangers?
- Are there other ways to get the same enjoyment that are legal?
- What are the risks of 'just having a go'?

At Key Stage 2, children will become increasingly aware of a variety of different media, and it is important that they explore how each medium presents information. The activities in this section offer children the opportunity to question this presentation, and to discover for themselves how both news and information may be managed.

SEEING THE WHOLE PICTURE

RESOURCES AND CLASSROOM ORGANISATION

You will need: photocopiable page 52, enlarged to A3 or displayed on an OHP; a large picture or poster that the children are already familiar with; paper and writing materials.

INTRODUCTION

Part of being a citizen is being able to have a critical view of information that we receive. Information from the media, particularly from the television, is often viewed as truth and fact rather than one reporter's interpretation of what they have seen or heard. Pictures on television and in newspapers, and images from the Internet, can appear to be a straightforward version of fact, but often these only portray part of a story shown from one person's (or groups) perspective or opinion.

This activity aims to give the children the awareness and skill to view information critically. It also helps them to question assumptions that we make about people and situations before evaluating the whole picture. They need to be aware of whether they are seeing the 'whole picture' or only part of it.

WHAT TO DO

To introduce the idea of only providing half the picture, give the children 'half a command' leaving out an important detail, such as *You are going to miss playtime… (…if you have two antennae coming out of your head)*. Explain to the children what you have just done and illustrate it by providing the other half of the command that you did not say. Emphasise to the children how important it is to know the whole command before you do something, otherwise, they would all have missed playtime!

Explain that this applies to many things, stories, pictures and real-life situations. Next show the children a picture or poster that they are familiar with, such as an advertisement or information poster in school, but cover up one half of it. Ask what they can see from one half, ask them also what they know to be hidden. Get the children with talk partners to discuss three things that have been missed off now that half the picture is hidden. Ask the class what they feel is the most important thing that is hidden. (The children will have different ideas, value all of them.)

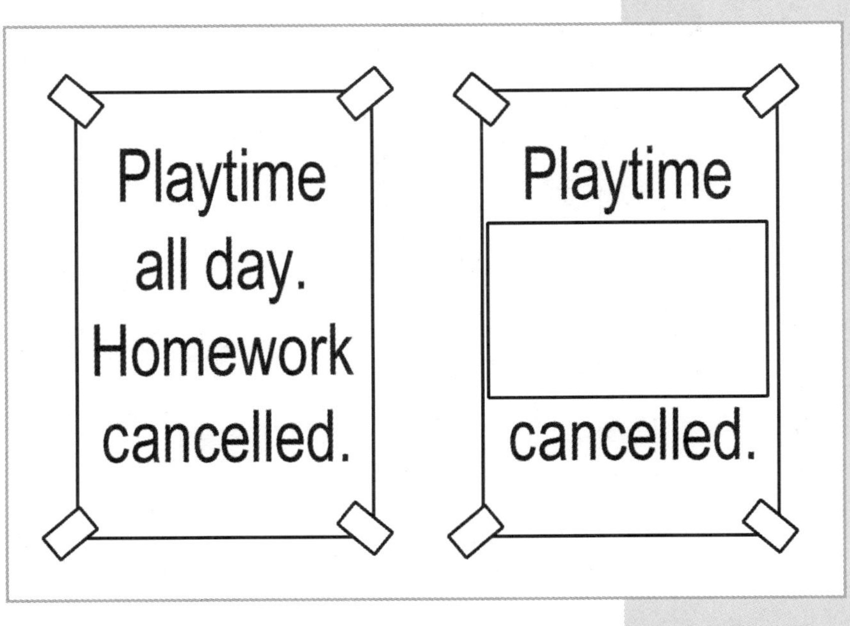

OBJECTIVES

To enable children to:
- understand that information from the media doesn't always show the whole picture
- realise the need to know the whole story before making judgements
- realise that information can be interpreted in different ways.

CROSS-CURRICULAR LINKS

HISTORY
Understanding that events can be represented and interpreted in different ways.

ENGLISH
Considering information critically, and distinguishing between fact and opinion.

Now explain that they are going to do the same process with an unfamiliar picture. Display photocopiable page 52 on the OHP, covering it so only part of the picture shows, for example the part just showing the boy running away with a purse in his hand or the shopkeeper shouting *Stop!* from his shop doorway.

Divide the class into groups of three or four. Ask them to discuss what they think might be happening in the whole picture. Tell them that they only have four minutes to do this. Request that one child is spokesperson from each group and lists the possible events occurring in the picture.

Next expose a new part of the picture to give more information about the events going on, for example the shopper with her bag open and things falling out. Ask the groups to evaluate the action again, now that they can see more of the picture. Ask them to think about what each character is doing in the picture and why they think the characters are doing it. For example, why is the boy running? Why has he got a purse in his hand? Whose purse is it? What is he going to do with it? How does this compare to the initial list of predictions? Have they changed their views about anyone's behaviour in the picture since they have seen more information? Can they predict what the final picture might show now?

Ask the groups to write down their prediction on a separate piece of paper and fold it up and then hand it to you. When all the predictions are collected, expose the final picture. Ask the children for their instant reactions. Now open some of the folded pieces of paper and compare them with what actually happens in the final picture.

Lead a class discussion about the children's assumptions of what was happening in the scene before they saw the whole picture. Did they think the shopkeeper was shouting after the woman or the boy running away with the purse? Did they presume the boy was stealing the purse? Why did they think that? Did anyone think he was helping the woman?

Conclusion

Relate the activity to pictures or reports in the media. How do we know if we are seeing the whole picture? Do we ever wonder what is happening behind the camera or just outside the frame of the camera picture?

How does this affect the truth of what we see on the television or hear on the radio? Who chooses what these things represent? Point out that we all interpret information and situations differently. It's good to wait until we have lots of information before making a judgement or assumption, and to be aware that information can be shown to us from one point of view only.

Now or later

■ Display the partly covered version of the picture and the children's predictions and comments on the classroom wall, and invite other children to come and look. Do they agree with the ideas displayed? Do they have the same predictions or different ones?

■ Use a piece of television footage (for example, a sports game or news report) and ask the class to evaluate it. What do they think they are not seeing? What would they like to see that the camera is not showing them?
■ When the children have had experience of evaluating several pictures, ask them to find or draw their own ambiguous picture. Emphasise that it doesn't have to be an unusual picture but one that has plenty of action in it. To develop the idea further, ask what can not be seen or what might be just out of the range of the picture.

READ ALL ABOUT IT!

RESOURCES AND CLASSROOM ORGANISATION

You will need: copies of photocopiable page 53, and the same sheet either enlarged to A3 or displayed on an OHP; a variety of daily newspapers (broadsheet, tabloid, local (including local free papers), regional and national) – it is important that these newspapers are at least likely to cover some of the same stories; flip chart or board.

The activity can quite easily be adapted to work for individuals, pairs or groups. If you are buying the newspapers yourself, you may want to opt for slightly larger groups. It will also be possible for each group to pass a newspaper on when they have finished looking for their particular story.

INTRODUCTION

This activity can be pitched at children across the Key Stage 2 age group. A more sophisticated analysis would obviously be expected of Year 6 children. If you wanted to look at a particular news story, you might want to use the previous day's newspapers, after you have found some good examples of a news item being dealt with in different ways.

WHAT TO DO

Ask the children if they know what stories are in the news at the moment. Write a list on the flip chart of all their suggestions. This should be a quick brainstorming session, so try to write down as many ideas as possible at this stage without commenting or vetting any suggestions. Next, narrow the list down to those items that are likely to feature in today's newspapers.

Show the children a variety of newspapers. Choose one headline story and show how it is represented in the different newspapers. Ask the children for their suggestions at this point. If they need help, ask them direct questions. *How big is the headline? How big is the photograph? How much of the page is given over to that particular story?* Now show the children your copy of photocopiable page 53. Demonstrate how the grid is to be completed.

Split the class into groups. Decide which group will be looking for which news story. Each group should then be given one or two newspapers to discover how that story is covered. After a reasonable amount of time, perhaps ten minutes, when they have completed the details in the grid, the groups should swap newspapers and continue to fill in their grid. Groups will need additional copies of the photocopiable sheet if they examine more than four newspapers.

When the children have searched all available newspapers for the news stories and have completed their grids, they should come back together on the carpet to report back their findings.

OBJECTIVES

To enable children to:
■ explore how newspapers present news
■ find out how different newspapers approach the same events in different ways.

CROSS-CURRICULAR LINKS

ENGLISH
Drawing on different features of text, including print and image, to obtain meaning.

SCIENCE
Making comparisons and observations.

Conclusion

Ask the children to listen carefully to each other to see what, if any, conclusions can be drawn. Do they notice which newspapers cover which stories in more detail? Why do they think this might be? Do these have fewer or smaller pictures? Do they notice any links between the sort of newspaper (tabloids and broadsheet, for example) and the type of coverage? Do any *not* cover a story? Can they think of any reasons for this?

Now or later

■ A homework activity could involve the children carrying out a similar task, using an adapted grid. This time they could see how news stories are represented on the television or in some other medium. Children could note down how different channels (including both terrestrial and digital, if possible) covered a story. This could be a collaborative project, in that different children monitor the coverage of *one* story across different channels/stations. They could then collate the results before presenting them to the rest of the class.
■ In groups, give the children a different news story to follow and questions to focus on, such as how long a story stays in the news.

The hottest seat

Objectives

To enable children to:
■ consider social and moral dilemmas that they come across in life
■ realise there are different kinds of responsibilities, and that these can sometimes conflict with each other.

Cross-curricular links

English/Drama
Using hot-seating techniques to explore characters and issues.

Resources and classroom organisation

You will need: flip chart or board; a variety of newspapers; a chair, which should be placed so that all the other children can clearly see the person sitting in it.

Introduction

This activity uses the hot-seating drama technique. In its simplest form, a character (a child or teacher in role) sits in a chair and has to answer questions as the character would answer. The other children in turn must ask the character questions, probing to find motivation and reasons for actions. The activity requires some children who are capable of concentration and careful, quick thought. It also means that the rest of the class can join in a drama activity without feeling threatened or pressured to perform. They can ask searching questions, with what some might feel is the benefit of relative anonymity. In this instance the character being questioned is the editor of a newspaper, and the children are trying to find out about the responsibilities involved in that particular role.

What to do

Show the children a recent newspaper featuring a controversial story. (Plan the activity far enough in advance for you to have had the chance to find a suitable story.) The story might be controversial because it raises issues about the private lives of people in the public eye, such as football players or pop stars. Ask the children whether they think it fair that such a story should be covered in the newspapers. Is it an invasion of privacy, or do people who make their living from the public, and who usually want publicity, have an obligation to accept what newspapers write about them, good or bad? Encourage the children to discuss these issues, and to give their justification for their viewpoints.

Tell the children that they are going to ask the editor of the newspaper why she decided to print that story. Explain that the editor is in charge of the newspaper and decides what is or is not included in it. Choose two or three volunteers to act as editors in the hot seat. Explain that when someone sits in the hot seat they must answer as the editor would answer. Try to find children who are likely to offer different responses – possibly someone who will be adamant that it was right to print the story, someone who is believes it was wrong, and someone who will waver when the children ask questions.

Now tell the editors they have a few minutes to think about how they will represent themselves when questioned. Similarly the rest of the children have that time to work out some testing questions for the editors. These questions should be based on the newspaper story looked at earlier. A child might ask the editor if she would have printed the same story if it had involved a relative of the editor's. Would the editor still have printed the story if there were no pressure to sell more copies of the newspaper? They may write their questions down on paper if you think this will help them.

Put each of the editors in the hot seat, in turn. Encourage the rest of the class to ask them questions. If you feel the children need help, you always have the option of asking a question yourself, but this choice should only be taken up if absolutely necessary.

Conclusion

Bring the class back together and discuss the editors' responses to the questions. Ask the children what sort of responsibilities people in the public eye, and those who write about them, have. Talk about the problem of conflicting responsibilities. For example, an editor may choose not to print a story about a public figure's love life on moral grounds, but the other newspapers may still print it and the editor's newspaper will sell fewer copies (and the public will still know about the public figure's love life). What would the children consider printing in a school newspaper?

Would they think it fair or reasonable to include an article about children who had been in trouble? Would it be a good idea to 'name and shame' other children in the school? What about printing photos from a Valentine's Disco where a shy boy had been seen giving a girl a Valentine's card – would it be fair to print such a photo? Other children would be very interested to see it, but it might embarrass the boy and girl in question.

Discuss any other conflicts of interest the children can think of that they may come across at school or home.

Now or later

The hot-seating technique has a variety of different uses across the curriculum, and is particularly useful in English and history. For example, in English a character from a story can be asked why they did what they did (Why did Little Red Riding Hood wander off the path? Why did Jack sell the cow for some magic beans?). In history, Julius Caesar could be asked why he invaded Britain, or Montezuma could be asked how he felt when he first saw the Spaniards, for example.

Who calls the shots?

Objectives

To enable children to:

- explore how the media presents information through photographs
- that there are different ways to portray the same event
- that the presentation of a photograph can manipulate our responses.

Cross-curricular links

English

Using character to convey story and emotions in drama.

History

Recognising how events can be represented in different ways.

Resources and classroom organisation

You will need: photocopiable page 54, one for each group of four children; a selection of photographs showing the same news event from different newspapers.

Introduction

Part of citizenship is building up skills to evaluate the reliability and truth of information that we receive. Recognising that images portrayed in the media have been presented in a specific way to manipulate our reactions is a vital part of this. In this activity the children role-play the jobs in different newspaper departments, so that they can see how events are portrayed in different ways to create different impressions.

What to do

Tell the children that today they are going to investigate what is behind the pictures that they see in newspapers. Have the selection of photographs from different newspapers ready to show and discuss these with the class. What is the main event that seems to be happening? Who do they think took the photo? Who would find the photo interesting? Does a photo of the same event taken by someone else show a very different picture? Tell the class that in this session they are going to be thinking about these questions all the time. To do this they are going to be in a role-play.

Explain that they are photographers working for an important newspaper (you could say this with you in role as the boss of the newspaper, sitting at your 'office desk') and that they will be covering an important news story. Ask the children to get into groups of four. Appoint, or draw lots to nominate, one child as photographer for each group.

Explain that the rest of the group will be the photograph: they will make a tableau or freeze-frame of the characters involved in the news event. It will be up to the photographer (with the help of their group) to decide what each character is doing, as well as the facial expression and attitude of each member of the group. The photographer can also choose to take 'close-ups' or 'wide-angled' shots or even decide on the angle they will hold the (pretend) camera at.

Having explained what they have to do, make it clear that whilst the news event will be the same, the photographers each come from different departments of the newspaper: the gossip column, headlines, arts and entertainment, and the news department. Each photographer will be expected to produce a photograph that matches the focus of their department.

Give one role-playing card (from photocopiable page 54) to each photographer. Then read out the news story that has just 'broken' (the bottom half of the photocopiable sheet). Give the children time to move to a small working space and start to construct their tableau directed by their photographer. Encourage them to think about how the photographer can choose parts of the tableau to match the style needed for their department. For example, facial expressions, the turn of a head, even someone scratching their nose can all influence the impression given by a photograph.

After about ten minutes, count down to *Freeze*. Unfreeze all but one group and ask each group in turn to 'present' their tableau. As they present it ask the other groups: *What department do you think their photographer comes from? What clues made you think that?* Each group must justify their answers.

Conclusion

Ask the class which part of the activity was the easiest to do and which was the hardest. Then ask them to compare the different ways that the photo was set up. Can they see how the same event can be presented in different ways? In what ways, and how, did the different departments represent the event? How did this affect the way readers might view the event?

Discuss how these questions apply to real newspapers and how sometimes what we see in the newspaper is just one way of looking at a story. Maybe it depends on what type of emphasis the editors or department bosses want from the photograph. Ask the class to have a second look at the newspaper photographs they viewed at the beginning of the lesson to see if there could be other ways of representing the same photograph.

Now or later

- If possible, use a digital or Polaroid camera to take the photographs and create a display. Ask the children to write (still in role as their respective departments) captions for their photographs.
- Collect together photographs and captions from newspapers and put them in a book called 'Who calls the shots – thoughts from our media experts!' Ask the children to bring in their own choice of photographs and let the other children guess what department the photographer might work for.

Name Date

Seeing the whole picture

Name Date

Read all about it!

Story	Title of paper	Is the story in the paper? If so, which page is it on?	Headline	How many pages are given to the story?	Photograph?

Name Date

Who calls the shots?

Headlines Department

You need to take eye-catching photographs that show drama and action.

Gossip Column

You should take photographs that show some juicy gossip.

News Department

You need to take photographs that sum up the main event and the background.

Arts and Entertainment Department

You should take action-packed and glamorous photographs.

NEWSFLASH>>>>NEWSFLASH>>>>NEWSFLASH>>>>

The pop group Shizzy Do were greeted by fans and reporters as they made their way to one of the country's biggest centres for homeless people today. The centre provides advice and training for those sleeping rough. Tonight Shizzy Do are going to perform free to raise money for homeless people.

NEWSFLASH>>>>NEWSFLASH>>>>NEWSFLASH>>>>

Section 7 TACKLING BULLYING AND RACISM

Combating bullying and racism is an important aim for every school. Whilst it can be hard to know where to start or whether the right thing is being said or done it is vital that teachers are seen to be addressing racism and bullying so that children have a clear message that bullying and racism are unacceptable. To combat bullying and racism most effectively many types of approaches should be used to match the different personalities and learning styles of children (and adults), a selection of which are provided here.

BANNER OF UNIQUENESS

RESOURCES AND CLASSROOM ORGANISATION

You will need: flip chart or board; paper and writing materials; measuring tapes.

The children work as individuals or in pairs, then go round the whole class comparing their ideas with each other. Organise the class in a way that suits you and have either a formal exchange of information with you telling the class when to move on to the next child, or an informal exchange where the children identify for themselves how they share the information.

INTRODUCTION

As a chosen part of an anti-racist strategy in school, celebrating diversity is an invaluable approach. The activity here involves the children finding out one or more things that are unique to them. It is meant to be fun and amusing whilst making the point clear.

WHAT TO DO

Introduce the concept of uniqueness either by personal example such as *I am unique in this room because I am over 25* or *I drive a car*. Go on to explain to the children that you are not unique within the school though, and to be unique in the world you would have to find something that only you have and no one else in the world has. Identifying your parents could be an example of this if you are an only child.

Tell the class that they are going to play a game to find ways in which they are unique in the class and possibly in the world. Give the class some categories (writing the headings on a flip chart) that they might use to find their own unique features or facts about themselves, for example:

- **body measurements** such as length of thumb or middle finger, length of stride, or circumference of wrist
- **family** such as where parents were born, stories from family history
- **interests and hobbies**, particularly any unusual ones.

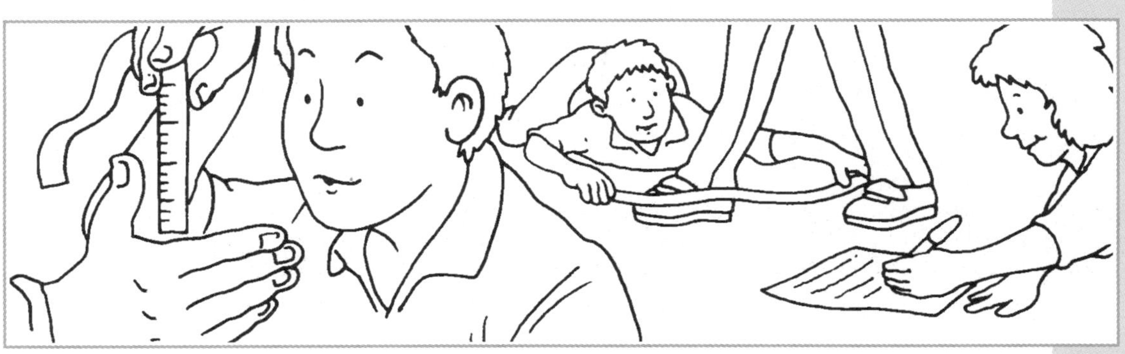

OBJECTIVES

To enable children to:

- appreciate that we are all unique and that this is a source of pride
- understand that ridiculing someone about their unique features or interests is wrong.

CROSS-CURRICULAR LINKS

SCIENCE

Making comparisons and measurements.

My unique facts	
Fact	**Detail**
Unusual hobby	I collect keys
The length of my thumb	4cm

When the class has plenty of ideas, tell them that they are each going to put together their own factsheet of ways in which they think they are unique. They should aim to have between five and ten facts and should record them in a style similar to that above (you could copy the table onto the flip chart for the children to see). If they need help with the measuring they could pair up with a work partner.

Give them fifteen minutes to complete their factsheets before bringing them back together again. Tell the children to work their way round the class, comparing their unique facts with each other to check off any similarities. Make it clear that having similarities is fine and there are plenty of opportunities for uniqueness.

Conclusion

When all the children have swapped their information, ask them to turn to a talk partner and discuss the following questions: *What does it feel like to be unique? Why do you like/not like it? What would it feel like if someone made fun of the thing that is unique about them?*

After three minutes return to a whole-class format. Ask the class if they can think of times when they do make fun of someone's uniqueness and bully them because of it. What do the class think about that and what do they think the person who is being made fun of thinks? Remind the class of the words *bullying* and *racism* and link this into the discussion. Emphasise that being unique is always something to be proud of, not ashamed; it is having something that no one else has.

Now or later

- The children could express their uniqueness as a banner with their own drawings/paintings on it or as a class book with individual unique pages for each person.
- The 'Weaving our lives' activity in the Diversity and community section links in well with this activity.

Appendix

- The anti-bullying campaign can be contacted on 020 7378 1446.
- Childline's website is at www.childline.org
- The Council for Racial Equality can be contacted at www.cre.gov.uk

Challenging prejudice

Resources and classroom organisation

You will need: one copy of photocopiable page 62 for each group of four children; writing materials.

Introduction

Whilst Britain is a diverse community, many of us have little knowledge of what many people in the community experience. This activity helps children to start to understand that some people are disadvantaged by circumstance and that this overspills into how they are viewed and treated by others. Stereotyping often leads to prejudice and misconceptions, and this activity aims to challenge this.

What to do

Introduce the idea that there are lots of different sorts of people living in one community. Ask the children to give you some examples – they may suggest old people or children. Suggest others to them, such as homeless people and consider how these people may live a different sort of life to the children. Be sensitive to all children in the class and their home lives/experiences. Tell the children that in this activity they are going to explore how people in different circumstances in the community are sometimes viewed negatively.

Split the class into groups of four and give each group a copy of photocopiable page 62. Ask them to consider the questions down the side of the table for each of the people along the top. They should write in their answers after discussing each situation. They can write yes, no or don't know in each space, or place a tick, a cross or a question mark there. They should concentrate on working on one person at a time, working their way down the list of questions so that they try and understand what that person's life is like, and what basic advantages and disadvantages each has in society. After a few minutes, stop the class and ask for some feedback. Point out that for a lot of the questions it may be impossible for us to know the answer, for instance whether an old person has qualifications or not, or whether a disabled person has a job.

Let the groups go back to work, and when they have finished ask each group to read out their answers, again taking a person from the sheet at a time so that comparison is made easier. The focus should be on each person's experience rather than on the housing or voting issues themselves. Discuss some of the issues with the children. There will probably be some instances where they may have made assumptions. For instance, they might assume that a traveller wouldn't have qualifications. Point out that some people choose to lead a nomadic lifestyle and that they may well have lots of qualifications, or a job. When you have worked your way through the list, ask the class if there are some things which they have learnt that they did not know before or if there is anything that surprises them.

Discuss any people that came out with a lot of crosses against them (approach this sensitively if there are travellers, refugees or disabled children in the class; you may wish to adapt the photocopiable sheet in these cases). Challenge the class if you think it appropriate and if they have made assumptions based on stereotyping, such as assuming that a refugee won't have qualifications (they may have been a doctor in their country of origin). Although there are some right or wrong answers, such as

Objectives

To enable children to:

- realise that in a diverse community some people are disadvantaged
- understand that some parts of the community are not listened to as much as others
- recognise that prejudice against some disadvantaged people in the community can come about through stereotyping and to begin to challenge this.

Cross-curricular links

English

Making contributions relevant to the topic and taking turns in discussion.

refugees not having the right to vote (it is also worth noting here that homeless people can now vote, as they can register at libraries), the idea is to challenge the children's stereotyping.

Appendix

■ Shelter provide resources specially designed for use in primary school, for general enquiries contact them on 020 7505 4699.
■ Disability Rights Commission: www.drc-gb.org
■ Gypsy Council for Education, Culture and Welfare Rights at 8 Hall Road, Aveley, Essex.

Conclusion

Focus on the final question on the photocopiable sheet and stress that because some parts of the community don't have the same rights or advantages as others this doesn't mean that they shouldn't be respected or listened to. Point out that everyone has a right to be listened to and to be treated fairly, because everyone is part of the community.

Now or later

Make a display or information booklet about inequality in our society with suggestions about what could be done to make our society a fairer place.

Roots of racism

Objective

To enable children to:
■ appreciate how the slave trade contributed to present-day racism.

Cross-curricular links

Mathematics

Making mental estimates for calculations.

History

Understanding how the past influences the present and learning about an aspect of British history in a wider world context.

Geography

Locating places and following routes.

Resources and classroom organisation

You will need: one enlarged copy of photocopiable page 63 for each group of three children; dice and counters; paper (to be used as recording sheets); writing materials.

Introduction

Because racism exists in our society, it is important that we provide the history about how and why the situation came about. In this activity an historically accurate board game simulates the slave trade in order that children can gain an insight into the way that West Africans were once treated by Europeans and Americans, and how the repercussions of these attitudes are still experienced in our modern-day society. It is important that the children have an opportunity to be each character in turn when they play the game to experience the slave trade from all points of view.

What to do

Tell the children that they are going to learn about one way in which racism and bullying happened in the history of Britain. Tell them that it is not a very nice story.

Recount the history of the English slave trade to the children, focusing on how this trade formed a triangle. Slave traders started out from England with relatively empty ships. In West Africa (which is now Sierra Leone, Ghana), slaves were bought and shipped straight to the West Indies and the southern half of the United States (as it is now). Here they were sold to the sugar plantation owners. Ships were then filled with valuable sugar and the slave traders set sail for England to sell the crops for huge profits. This triangular trading pattern flourished for three hundred years devastating the population of West Africa and accumulating huge fortunes for the plantation owners and the English companies running the boats.

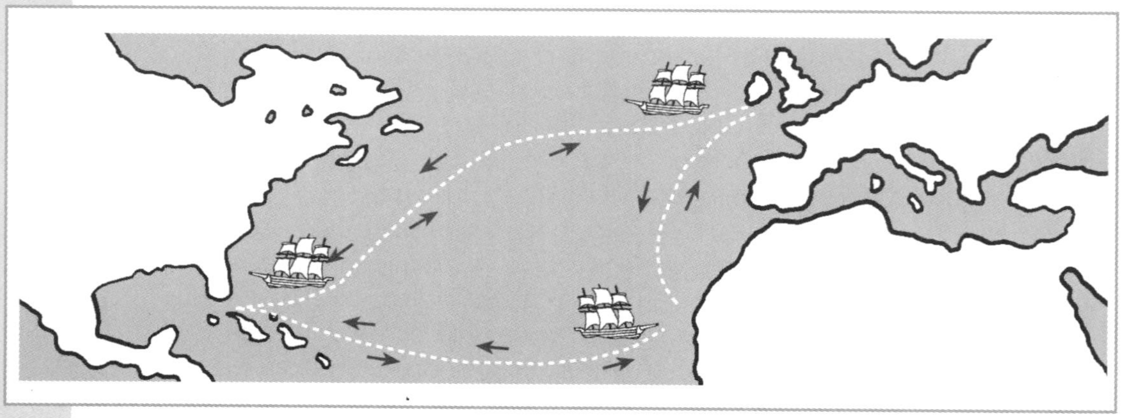

Section 7

Tell the children that now they are going to play a game to see who benefited from the slave trade and who didn't. Put the children into groups of three and ask them to roll the dice to see who plays which character. The child that rolls the lowest number plays the slave trader, the middle number plays the plantation owner and the highest number plays the slave. Give out a copy of the board game to each group of three children and the paper to be used as recording sheets. Each character has a marked starting place on the board and a different set of squares showing how their part in the slave triangle works. The different squares that the character lands on will give different instructions. Both the slave trader and the plantation owner will be told to borrow money (their industries were seen as very good investments). To borrow money they should write down the amount borrowed on their recording sheet. Explain to the children that profit is the amount of money they have left after having bought the slaves (money spent) and the money made by either selling on the slaves (the slave traders) or selling the sugar crop (the plantation owners). They should work out their total profits at the end of the game.

The slave trader, having accumulated enough money in England, sails to Africa. Here he uses whatever money he has to buy slaves (at £20 a slave). When the character reaches the end of the circle of squares he has to set sail for the West Indies with the ship's hold full of slaves. On reaching the West Indies the slave trader now sells the slaves, using the selling price list in the top-left corner of the sheet, and notes this down on the recording sheet. The slave trader then returns to Africa and repeats the buying slaves circuit. The trader's profit can be worked out at the end of the game.

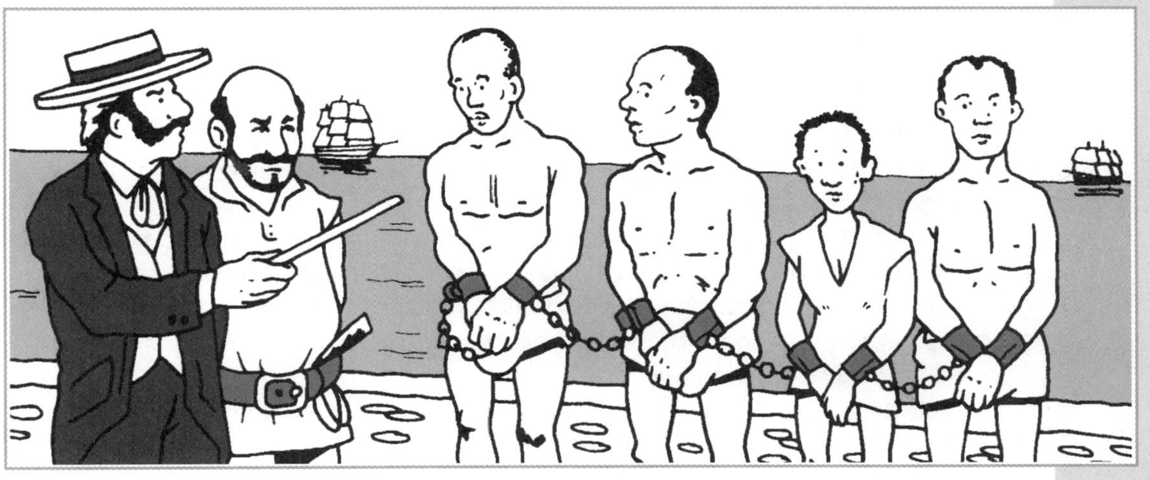

The plantation owner starts by borrowing money and buying slaves. The sugar crop can be harvested when that square is reached and he has 750 slaves. (He should keep going around the West Indies circuit until he has collected 750 slaves. He should also note down if any of his slaves have died and needs to buy more to replace them.) To sell the sugar the plantation owner's boat sails to England. After the sale the plantation owner returns to the West Indies, showing how the money is returned to the plantations. When the owner returns he can move round the circle again but this time he does not have to spend money on slaves, so all the profit from the harvest can go onto the recording sheet.

The slaves start in Africa and are transported to the West Indies. Players may land on 'dying' squares on this voyage. If so, they go back to the start and start again. Once in the West Indies they follow their own track of work, or land on 'flogging' or 'dying' squares. As each slaves dies or gets flogged they record each on the recording sheet, going back to the start each time they die.

Make sure that all children have had a chance to play each character (place a time limit of, say, 15 minutes for each game) and then bring the class back together. Discuss the experience of the different characters. Which character made the most money? What was the experience of the slave? What do they think about the concept of being bought or someone owning another human being? Make it clear that whilst they were playing a game these events really happened, and the deaths in the game represent real deaths and real people being taken from their families.

Appendix

- *Black and British* by David Bygott (Oxford University Press) has a very clear account of the slave trade and shows how it affected Britain.
- *Slavery from Africa to the Americas* by Christine Hatt (Evans Brothers) is a useful reference book.

Conclusion

A significant aspect of slavery was the way people thought about black people at that time. In order to make themselves feel better about treating people in such a terrible way, the whites persuaded themselves that the black slaves were less than human. This led to a picture of African cultures as inferior to white cultures. This is the basis of much of historical white racism. This is a difficult point to put over to children, but will be made easier once they have played the game and experienced a hint of the lack of respect shown by the slave traders and plantation owners.

Now or later

Children could decide on ways to represent what they have learnt about the slave trade and their reaction to it. This could take the form of poetry, posters, leaflets or information booklets.

Beating bullying

Objectives

To enable children to:

- understand the nature and consequences of racism, teasing, bullying and aggressive behaviours
- learn about ways of responding to bullies and how to ask for help.

Cross-curricular links

English/Drama

Using dramatic techniques to explore characters and issues; using narrative to convey ideas in plays they both devise and script.

Resources and classroom organisation

You will need: flip chart or board; paper; writing materials.

After working as a whole class, the children will write and perform in small groups – three or four in each group is ideal. The children will need somewhere to write, but the space must also be arranged so that the scenes can be presented to the rest of the class.

Introduction

This is a very demanding activity and is probably most suitable for those children at the top end of Key Stage 2. It requires a mature and sensible approach from the children. As with most activities that deal with issues of this kind, it is recommended that it is not used as a way of dealing with a problem that has arisen, but rather as part of an ongoing programme which addresses such concerns. Its aim is to encourage children to spot potential problems, and to give them strategies to deal with such problems should they arise.

This activity gives the children opportunities to make suggestions about what they can say or do when faced with various difficult situations, such as bullying. Bullying can range from infrequent name-calling to persistent physical aggression – and all of it needs to be dealt with immediately.

What to do

Begin a discussion about the reasons children get picked on at school. Write down the different scenarios the children suggest on a flip chart. Stress that the scenarios do not have to be from personal experience. They may have heard of other people who have been bullies or bullied.

Run through one of the scenarios from the flip chart as an example with the whole class. Can the children think of a safe and sensible way to respond to this particular instance of bullying? For example, if a child was being called names, possible ways of responding could include ignoring the name-calling, telling the bully that you are not bothered by the name-calling, asking the bully why they are calling you names, or telling an adult. Which, if any, of these do the children think would be a good idea and why? How do they think the bully will react to these options? Explain that there is not a right or wrong answer, but it is important that all children and adults work together to combat bullying.

Split the children into small groups and tell them to write a scene based on one of the bullying incidents from the list on the flip chart, including a way to deal with the situation. Explain that the scene should be in a playscript format so that they can each take a part and perform it to the rest of the class. Emphasise that the scenes should be short, simple and offer a realistic comment. Tell the children that what they are doing is difficult and sophisticated. This is not an activity that younger children could cope with, but they are now mature enough to consider such situations.

After a suitable amount of time, say ten or fifteen minutes, tell the groups to rehearse their scenes before showing them to the other members of the class. You can decide whether certain members of the class – those with reading difficulties or children who are not confident speaking in front of others – can choose a different way of presenting. They might present a tableau showing stages of a scene, rather than acting it out.

Bring the children back together and prepare the classroom or other space for the presentation of the scenes. Explain that acting skills are not the most important point. What you want to see is the issue and that it has been clearly addressed. Encourage the children to get into the habit of showing appreciation for this sort of work by clapping and/or offering positive comments after each presentation.

When all the scenarios have been presented, ask the children how they think people have been affected in each scene, and whether they dealt well with the situation they faced. Do they think the person being bullied has come out of the situation feeling stronger? Is it possible that the bully might change her behaviour because of what has been said?

Conclusion

Emphasise that it is very important that the children think about different strategies for dealing with difficult situations. The children need to learn that different tactics might be fitting in different situations. For instance, would you respond differently to being bullied by someone from your class or by someone you don't know? Is it easier to seek help from your classroom teacher, for example, if you know the bully? Would it be possible to seek help from older children in your school? Suggest it might be a good idea to set up a scheme where the responsible older children in the school could act as monitors to keep an eye on the younger children, and to act as a go-between between the children and adults.

Talk about the consequences of bullying. What do the children think can happen after someone has been bullied? Do they have an idea why people bully? Again, be clear that you are not asking the children to talk about particular people, though they may, if you feel confident in this area, talk about personal experiences. Mention any initiatives that you have heard or read about, such as whole school days focusing on anti-bullying, writing anti-bullying policies with the children, or even something as simple as making friendship bracelets for the younger children.

Now or later

- When the children have become competent at writing short scenes, they might want to swap with other groups – that is, write scenes for the other groups to act out. This involves different, and a higher order of, interpretative skills.
- The children can move on to writing their own script ideas for other situations and scenarios, which might deal with other issues aside from bullying. This sort of work would tie in well with looking at stories that raise issues in the Literacy Hour.

Name Date

Challenging prejudice

	Old person	Homeless person	Disabled person	Traveller/ gypsy	Refugee	Employee
Do they have a home?						
Can they vote?						
Do they have a job?						
Do they have qualifications?						
Do they enjoy good health?						
Are they listened to and respected?						

Name Date

Roots of racism

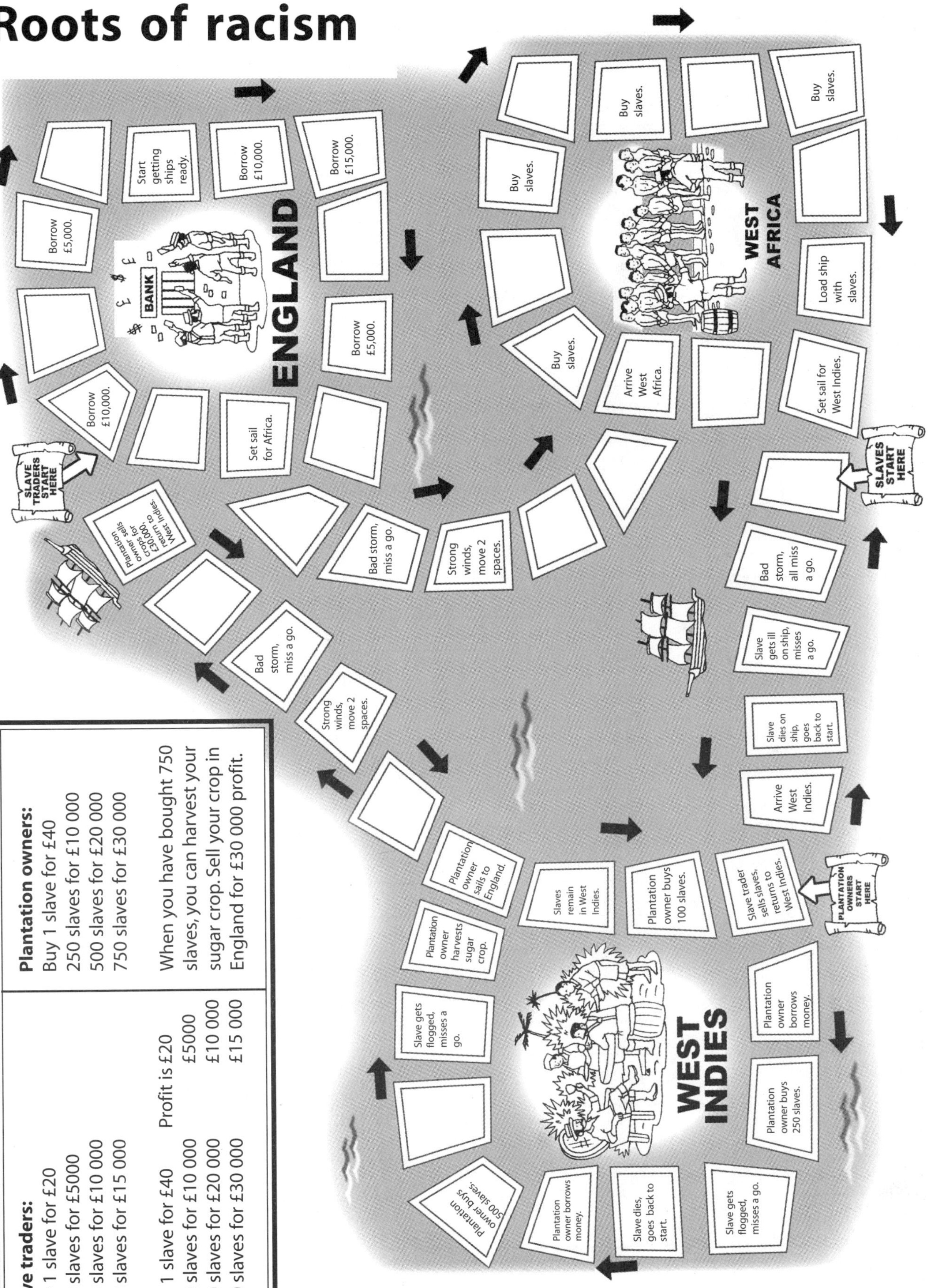

Slave traders:		Plantation owners:
Buy 1 slave for £20		Buy 1 slave for £40
250 slaves for £5000		250 slaves for £10 000
500 slaves for £10 000		500 slaves for £20 000
750 slaves for £15 000		750 slaves for £30 000
Sell 1 slave for £40	Profit is £20	When you have bought 750 slaves, you can harvest your sugar crop. Sell your crop in England for £30 000 profit.
250 slaves for £10 000	£5000	
500 slaves for £20 000	£10 000	
750 slaves for £30 000	£15 000	

Skills Grid

National Standards for Key Skills

Activity	Learning themes	Skills	Page
Shades of opinion	Opinions are not always clear cut	Discussing, debating, justifying opinions	5
Viewfinder	Accessing relevant information from text	Research skills, scanning texts	6
Implications game	Exploring different implications of information	Thinking logically, inference	8
The CHECK test	Evaluating the reliability of information	Thinking critically, asking questions	9
Weaving our lives together	Appreciating diversity in communities	Reflecting, working together, communicating ideas through art	11
Celebration pot	Recognising and developing qualities and skills	Playing co-operatively, thinking skills, communicating ideas through art	12
Hidden history	The cultural diversity of British history	Playing a game, reflecting, working together	14
'Take a seat, please...'	Reflecting on own skills and thinking about future careers	Role-playing, working together	15
Familiar families?	The diversity of family make-ups	Reflecting, working together, communicating ideas through art	17
The pledge tree	Actions affect the environment	Making shapes and cutting out, generating ideas, making decisions	19
Traffic calmer	Road safety	Problem-solving, justifying decisions	21
Fuel bill mystery	The school's impact on the environment	Thinking logically, problem-solving, justifying opinions	22
Transport chaos	The need for balance in the environment	Playing a game, scientific thinking	24
Action stations	The role of local and national government	Playing a game, discussing	28
Soapbox corner	Debating topical issues	Explaining and justifying opinions, asking questions	30
Rights	Children's rights	Using mime to explore issues	31
You can save the world!	Analysing problems and considering solutions	Brainstorming, drawing up action plans	33
It's your choice!	Actions have consequences that affect others	Playing a game, thinking logically	35
Thinking about feelings	Exploring emotions	Dramatising scenarios with puppets	37
Roll the dice	Resolving differences by looking at alternatives	Problem-solving, considering solutions	38
Making smart choices	Making choices based on reliable information	Sorting and assessing information	39
Seeing the whole picture	Information can be interpreted in different ways	Sorting and assessing information	45
Read all about it!	The representation of information by the media	Evaluating information, asking questions, working together	47
The hottest seat	Responsibilities can conflict with interests	Role-playing (hot-seating), asking and answering questions	48
Who calls the shots?	Information manipulation by the media	Generating, discussing and justifying ideas, mime	50
Banner of uniqueness	Celebrating diversity	Exchanging information, communicating through art	55
Challenging prejudice	Stereotypes	Playing a game, working together	57
Roots of racism	The contribution of the slave trade to present-day racism	Playing a game, empathising	58
Beating bullying	Understanding and tackling bullying and racism	Dramatising scenarios, working together and generating ideas	60